THE WAY OF THE WESLEYS

The Way of the Wesleys

A Short Introduction

John R. Tyson

WILLIAM B. EERDMANS PUBLISHING COMPANY
GRAND RAPIDS, MICHIGAN / CAMBRIDGE, U.K.

Published 2014 by

Wm. B. Eerdmans Publishing Co.

2140 Oak Industrial Drive N.E., Grand Rapids, Michigan 49505 /

P.O. Box 163, Cambridge CB3 9PU U.K.

Printed in the United States of America

20 19 18 17 16 15 14   7 6 5 4 3 2 1

Library of Congress Cataloging-in-Publication Data

ISBN 978-0-8028-6954-8

www.eerdmans.com

Contents

CONTENTS

Introduction

John (1703-91) and Charles Wesley (1707-88) are famous to most modern readers as the co-founders of the Wesleyan tradition and the Methodist family of churches. Their impact and legacy has been huge. What began as the excited outpouring of their conversion experiences grew into a transatlantic revival, and eventually became a vibrant and significant theological tradition. The inception of the Methodist movement was shaped profoundly by the unique gifts and graces of the Wesley brothers. But the staying power and popularity of the movement, as an expression of what the Wesleys called "vital Christianity," had to do with the theology and practices they crafted. It is to that inheritance that we turn our attention in the present volume.

Various historical depictions of the Wesley brothers are available to us. There is the evangelical and experiential view of them, as people whose hearts were "strangely warmed" in May 1738. The diminutive Oxford dons soon turned mass evangelists, and their prodigious efforts at addressing people who stood at the margins of eighteenth-century English society offer a second evangelistic depiction of them that is often measured in sermons preached (more than 40,000) or miles traveled on horseback (more than 250,000) or hymns produced (more than 9,000). In this vein, Albert Outler rightly styled John Wesley a "Folk Theologian," since Wesley described himself as one who "spoke plain words to plain folks," and prided himself in speaking *ad populum* ("to the common people"). The irony of John using a classical Latin phrase to describe his popular preaching style should remind us that he, like Charles, was a highly educated Christian minister who used his considerable gifts to translate complicated theological discourse for the common people. It was in this sense that Outler described John Wesley as a "popularizer" who intentionally concealed his learning. Or there is the picture of the Wesleys as social activists, a depiction so firmly based in their advocacy for the "working poor" that competent historians of the period, like Elie Halvey, have made the extravagant claim that the Wesleyan revival was instrumental in sparing England the violent revolution and social disorder that convulsed France during the same period under similar circumstances. Even the Wesleys' detractors have acknowledged their far-reaching influence and contributions, but lack of theological reflection and spiritual insight leaves their detractors at a loss when it comes to describing the source and foundation of the Wesleys' remarkable impact and accomplishments.

Of course, John Wesley had some disagreeable aspects to his personality. He was a highly motivated, determined, and sometimes domineering person who generally had a clear idea of what needed to be done and how to do it. When he was convinced that he or the Methodists were on "the right course" (as he believed God had given him to see the right), John Wesley was difficult to divert. His determined, autocratic style of leadership earned him the jibe "Pope John," and yet Wesley was approachable enough to be called to account for his leadership style at the Methodist Conference of 1766.

For his part, Charles Wesley had quite a temper. On one occasion his brother lamented: "How apt you are to take the color of your company! When you and I [talked] together you *seemed* at least to be of the same mind with me, and now you are all off the hooks again! . . . [U]nless you only talk because you are in the humor of contradiction; if that is so, I might as well blow against the wind as talk to you." Charles could and did sometimes act impetuously, without adequate regard for other people's feelings, as when he married off Grace Murray, the love of John Wesley's life, to another suitor. Both brothers could be stubborn and intransigent — particularly when dealing with each other.

Yet despite their emotional and personal differences, they were one in Christ and one in their formulation of the Wesleyan approach to Christian doctrine. They were also one in their profound sense of mission to the world. It was upon these foundations, and not their kinship alone, that the Wesley brothers forged a partnership in ministry that lasted more than five decades, and engendered a theological tradition that boasts more than seventy-five million adherents today.

My purpose in this introductory survey of Wesleyan theology is not to present John and Charles Wesley as cult heroes. Nor do I intend to combine the various popular portraits of the Wesleys to present them as "strangely warmed" evangelists, mystical poets, or social saviors. Each of these popular portraits of them is accurate to some degree — perhaps in the same way a caricature accurately captures a few of the prominent features of a person — and in that sense they remind us why the Wesleys are worth remembering. But none of these popular pictures adequately explains why the Wesleys continue to be valuable theological mentors to me as I go about the demanding tasks of trying to be a faithful follower of Jesus Christ.

As a church historian, I agree with Albert Outler that "John Wesley was the most important Anglican theologian of the eighteenth century because of his distinctive, composite answer to the age-old question as to 'the nature of the Christian life.' " Much the same could be and has been said of his lesser-known brother, Charles. In view of their historical significance alone, John and Charles Wesley deserve to be remembered and studied. But like so many others, I am a person who (to use the Wesleyan phrase) stands "in connection with Mr. Wesley"; for me, the Wesleys are spiritual guides who help me live out my Christian faith. They are theological mentors to whom I frequently turn and from whom I occasionally learn. What follows, then, is a theological assessment (instead of a purely historical one) of why I find John and Charles Wesley to be fellow Christians worth remembering — and perhaps more importantly, worth consulting as mentors in Christian faith and practice today.

CHAPTER ONE

We to the Sacred Standard Fly

THE BIBLE

Let me be *homo unius libri* [a man of one book].

John Wesley, Preface, *1746 Sermons*

John and Charles Wesley first encountered and absorbed the Bible in the little school that their mother, Susanna Annsley Wesley (1669-1742), conducted in their home in Epworth, England. All of the Wesley children were home-schooled through the primary grades, due largely to financial necessity, and they were taught to read from the premier literary work in their house — the Bible. At the tender age of five, each child was taught to read, by beginning in Genesis and working their way through the Bible, under mother's watchful eye and encouraging instruction. All the Wesley children were quick learners, including brothers John and Charles; by the end of his first day at school, young Charles could read the first chapter of Genesis quite well. The intervening years did nothing to dull their interest in and attention to the Bible.

John Wesley's writings point to the year 1729 as a watershed year with respect to his spiritual pilgrimage. It was the year of the founding of the Oxford Holy Club, that small group of devout college students who met together to discover and live out what they considered to be vital Christianity. John subsequently wrote, "In the year 1729 I began to not only read, but to study the Bible as the one and the only standard of truth, and the only model of pure religion." He made a similar point when recounting the history of the Methodist movement from the distance of many years: "What was their foundational doctrine? That the Bible is the whole and sole rule of both Christian faith and practice." That their fellow students noticed the Holy Club's attempts to adhere to biblical doctrines and practices was clear, since they reviled them with a barrage of nicknames: "supererogation men," "Bible moths," "Bible maggots" — and, of course, the one that stuck: "Methodists." In John's sermon "On God's Vineyard," he attributed the rise of the Oxford Methodists to their particular desire to be *homo unius libri:*

> From the very beginning, from the time that four young men united together, each of them was *homo unius libri* — a man of one book. God taught them all to make his word "a lantern unto their feet, and a light in all their paths." They had one and only one rule of judgment with regard to all their tempers, words, and actions; namely, the oracles of God. They were one and all determined to be Bible Christians. They were continually reproached for this very thing; some terming them in derision, Bible-bigots, others Bible-moths — feeding, they said, upon the Bible as moths do upon cloth, and indeed unto this day it is their constant endeavour to think and speak as [do] the oracles of God.

They were being lampooned for the way they sought to burrow into the Bible, to digest it methodically in order to live it out. Indeed, from those early days onwards, John Wesley professed that he wanted nothing more or less than to be a "Bible-Christian," who was part of a movement that was raised up by God to spread "Scriptural holiness across the land."

The Oracles of God

Their favorite euphemism for the Scriptures was "the oracles of God." The phrasing was borrowed from 1 Peter 4:11: "If any man speak, let him speak as the oracles of God." The term appears more than seventy times in John's published sermons and is seasoned throughout Charles's hymns and sermons as well. It stresses the revelatory impact that the brothers felt in the Scriptures; in them they heard the voice of God. Because of the deep interconnection between the Word and Spirit of God these were "living oracles," and a rule of faith by which doctrine, creed, and religious experience were all evaluated. As Charles wrote,

> Doctrines, experiences to try,
> We to the sacred standard fly,
> Assured the Spirit of Our Lord

Can never contradict His word;
Whate'er His Spirit speaks in me,
Must within the written word agree;
If not — I cast it all aside,
As Satan's voice, or nature's pride.

The test of truth and righteousness,
O God, Thy records we confess,
And who Thine oracles gainsay
Have miss'd the right celestial way:
Their pardon sure they vainly boast,
In nature sunk, in darkness lost;
Or if they of perfection dream,
The light of grace is not in them.

In the preface to his famous *Notes Upon the New Testament* John described what he meant by the inspiration of the Scriptures. He saw God, through the Holy Spirit, as the primary author of the Bible:

In the language of the sacred writings, we may observe the utmost depth, together with the utmost ease. All the elegancies of human composures sink into nothing before it: God speaks not as man, but as God. His thoughts are very deep; and thence his words are of inexhaustible virtue. And the language of his messengers, also, is exact in the highest degree: for the words which are given them accurately answered for the impression made upon their minds: And hence Luther says, "Divinity is nothing but a grammar of the language of the Holy Ghost."

After their conversion experiences in May 1738, neither Wesley brother was able to read the Bible in a lifeless, wooden sort of way. For both brothers the Bible was the story of God's salvation, as lively and exciting now as in the ancient days of its first rendition. It was in this sense that John, who was an omnivorous reader in many fields, was willing to style himself as *homo unius libri* — "a man of one book." As John wrote in the extensive preface to his 1746 collection of sermons:

I want to know one thing, the way to heaven. How to land safe on that happy shore. God himself has condescended to teach the way. For this very end he came from heaven. He hath written it down in a book. O

3

give me that Book! I have it. Here is enough knowledge for me. Let me be *homo unius libri.* Here I am far from the busy ways of men . . . only God is here. In his presence I open, I read his book, for this end, to find the way to heaven.

This Bible-centered emphasis continued throughout the Wesleys' lives and more than half a century in their ministry. As John wrote in his journal entry for June 2, 1766, "My ground is the Bible. Yea, I am a Bible-bigot. I follow it in all things, both great and small." Hence, Wesley's theology of proclamation amounted to plainly saying what the Bible said: "God himself told us how to speak, both as to the matter and the manner. 'If any man speak' in the name of God 'let him speak as the oracles of God.' "

It is hard to imagine anyone who has been as saturated with Scripture as the Wesley brothers were. Biblical phrases and allusions poured from them, not only in sermon and in song, but in the course of their casual speech and private writings. Hence, J. Ernest Rattenbury wryly observed in *The Evangelical Doctrines of Charles Wesley's Hymns,* "a skillful man, if the Bible were lost, might easily reconstruct it from Wesley's hymns. They contain the Bible in solution." The same thing could easily said of the Wesleys' sermons and letters. Their sermons are patchworks of biblical phrases and citations, and their hymns are mosaics of finely chosen biblical phrases and allusions cemented together to form a new theological whole. Kenneth Newport pointed out an example of this process in Charles's sermon on Romans 3:23-25, in which a single paragraph is made up of phrases and allusions to Matthew 9:12, Luke 5:32, Matthew 11:19, Romans 6:1, Romans 3:29, and Philippians 3:8. They studied and proclaimed the Bible using "the analogy of faith," which meant that Scripture was used to interpret Scripture. As John reported elsewhere, "by comparing spiritual things with spiritual, we may show the meaning of the oracles of God." And they read their Bible from the inner logic of the gospel of God's grace: "It is easily discerned," John wrote, "that these two little words — I mean faith and salvation — include the substance of all the Bible, the marrow as it were, of the whole Scripture." In the afterglow of their conversion experiences, the Wesleys' "Preface" to their *Hymns and Sacred Poems* (1739) gave expression to their Bible-centrism, as well as to the Bible's own call to social responsibility:

In every age and century Satan has whispered to those who began to taste the power of the world to come, "to the desert," "to the wilderness!" Most of our little flock at Oxford were tried with this; my brother and I in particular; nay, but I say, "to the Bible." "To the Bible," and there you will learn as you have time, "to do good to all men," to warn everyone, to exhort everyone as you have opportunity.

Reading the Scriptures was described as one of the "instituted means of grace," described in the "General Rules" which the Wesley brothers developed for the governance and practice of their Methodist Societies. They asked the Methodists if they were

> *Searching the Scriptures* by (i) reading, constantly, some part of [them] every day; regularly, all the Bible in order, carefully with the *Notes;* seriously with prayer before and after; fruitfully, immediately practicing what you learn there? (ii) meditating, at set times? By any rule? (iii) hearing: every morning? Carefully; with prayer before and after; immediately putting into practice? Have you a New Testament always about you?

The Scriptures were considered a "means of grace" because in reading them a person could meet God and Jesus Christ, by the power of the Holy Spirit, and experience God's revelatory and transforming message. As John wrote in his sermon on "The Means of Grace," "all who desire the grace of God are to wait for it in 'searching the Scriptures.' Our Lord's direction with regard to the use of this means is likewise plain and clear. 'Search the Scriptures,' saith he to the unbelieving Jews, 'for . . . they . . . testify of me.' And for this very end he direct[ed] them to search the Scriptures, that they might *believe in him.*" John's hymn on Matthew 9:20-21, where a woman is cured of a hemorrhage by touching the hem of Jesus' garment, expressed well the Wesleys' reverence for the Bible ("I blush and tremble to draw near"), and as well as their willingness to view the Scriptures as a "garment" through which "to touch my Lord":

> Unclean, of life and heart unclean,
> How shall I in His sight appear!
> Conscious of my inveterate sin
> I blush and tremble to draw near;
> Yet through the garment of His Word
> I humbly seek to touch my Lord.

The goal of this Scripture reading was the actualization of the text in human life. In his poetical comment on Revelation 1:3 ("Blessed is he that readeth") Charles reminded his reader that "the mystic words" illuminated by the Holy Spirit ("Divine Interpreter") become "Words that endless bliss impart" when "Kept in an obedient heart." His second stanza implies that the blessings of the Word are found in the hearing and the doing of it, since through hearing and doing the Word the Kingdom of God comes upon the earth and the glory of Christ is revealed — both now in and the Lord's return:

> Come, Divine Interpreter,
> Bring me eyes Thy book to read,
>   Ears the mystic words to hear,
> Words which did from Thee proceed,
>   Words that endless bliss impart,
> Kept in an obedient heart.
>
> All who read, or hear, are bless'd,
>   If Thy plain commands we do,
> Of Thy Kingdom here possess'd,
>   Thee we shall in glory view,
> (When Thou comest on earth to abide)
>   Reign triumphant at Thy side.

Writing in the Age of Reason and in the theological context of Deism, the Wesleys were well aware that fellow religionists did not share their Bible-centrism. In his sermon "On Faith," John Wesley averred that in his mind, the willingness to believe the Bible and its description of God's action in the world was a watershed between classical Christianity and Deism: "The second sort of faith, if you allow a materialist to have any, is the faith of a Deist. I mean he who believes there is a God, distinct from matter, but does not believe the Bible." In a similar way, Wesley's Bible-centrism committed him to a supernatural worldview, and a belief in miracles. Hence John's unnamed interlocutor in his sermon "On Providence" asked: "What! You expect miracles then?" "Certainly I do," Wesley replied, "if I believe the Bible. For the Bible teaches me that God answers prayer."

The theological and ethical use of the Bible lay at the core of the Methodist movement. The failure to hold to the centrality of the Bible, or a lack of fidelity to biblical norms, was — as John wrote in Sermon No. 122 — one of the chief "Causes of the Inefficacy of Christianity":

I am distressed. I know not what to do. I see what I might have done. I might have said peremptorily and expressly; "Here I am; I and my Bible. I am not, I dare not vary from this Book, either in great things or small. I have no power to dispense with one jot or tittle of what is contained therein. I am determined to be a Bible Christian, not almost, but altogether." Who will join me on this ground? Join me on this, or not at all.

We see this desire to be a "Bible Christian," who follows the Bible in "great things or small," at work in the Wesleys' doctrine and theological expressions. For example, John Wesley's Sermon No. 73, "Of Hell," avers that he finds contemplation of the torments of hell personally distasteful, but since he finds them in the Bible, they must be admitted to — though not exaggerated by human imagination: "surely this is too awful a subject to admit of such play of imagination. Let us keep to the written Word. It is terrible enough to dwell with everlasting burnings." Similarly, he wanted to follow biblical cues when speaking of the Trinity:

> I dare not insist upon anyone's using the word "trinity" or "person." I use them myself without any scruple, because I know of none better. But if any man has any scruple concerning them, who shall constrain him to use them? I cannot, much less would I burn a man alive — and that with moist, green wood, for saying "though I believe the Father is God, the Son is God, and the Holy Spirit is God, yet I scruple using the words 'trinity' and 'persons.'" *Because I do not find those terms in the Bible.*

In a similar way, the Wesleys were willing to use extravagant-sounding theological terms like "perfection" to describe their doctrine of sanctification because the Bible used it: "Therefore learning the principles of the doctrine of Christ, let us go on to perfection." John Wesley was so determined to use the language of the Bible that he did not want to use the word "dear" to refer to God, either in sermon, prayer, or song. In fact, when Charles would use "dear" this way, John tried to edit it out of Charles's hymns and poems.

Both John and Charles Wesley had unambiguous confidence in the accuracy of the Bible. About Soame Jenyns's "admired tract," *A View of the Internal Evidence of the Christian Religion,* John wrote, "He is undoubtedly a fine writer; but whether he is a Christian, deist, or atheist, I cannot tell. If he is a Christian, he betrays his own cause by averring that, 'All Scripture is not given by inspiration of God; but the writers of it were sometimes left to themselves and consequently made some mistakes.' Nay, if there be any mistakes in the Bible, there may as well be a thousand. If there be one falsehood in that book, it did not come from the God of truth." Charles's "Short Hymn" on 1 Peter 4:11 evidences this same confidence in the content and authority of the Scriptures:

1. Let all who speak in Jesu's name,
   To His submit their every word,
   Implicit faith in them disclaim,
   And send the hearers to their Lord;
   Who doth His Father's will reveal,
   The only Guide infallible.

2. Jesus, to me Thy mind impart,
   Be Thou Thine own Interpreter,
   Explain the Scripture to my heart,
   That when the church Thy servant hear,
   Taught by the oracles Divine,
   They all may own, the word is Thine.

While the Scriptures have supreme theological and ethical authority, these are located in the revelatory work of God's Spirit, who calls to mind the things of Christ (John 14:25-26), and bears witness to Christ (John 15:26). As Charles wrote,

1. The Scriptures never can be known
   But through the power of God alone;
   The Spirit of power, and truth, and love
   Doth first our unbelief remove,
   Discovers the deep things of God,
   And shows to me my Saviour's blood.

2. My Father's mind I then perceive,
   And quicken'd by His Spirit live;
   The Spirit doth His word reveal,
   The Spirit teaches me His will,
   And while into all truth He guides,
   My teacher in my heart resides.

Therefore those who would not be guilty of "Corrupting the Word of God," as John described it in his sermon by that title, must "publish, as proper occasions offer, all that is contained in the oracles of God: whether smooth or otherwise it matters nothing, since 'tis unquestionably true, and useful too. For 'all Scripture given by inspiration of God is profitable either for doctrine, or reproof, or correction, or instruction in righteousness' [2 Tim. 3:16]; either to teach us what we are to believe or practice; for conviction of error or reformation of vice. They know that there is nothing superfluous in it, relating to either faith or practice; and therefore they preach all parts of it." Those among his contemporaries who made "so small account of one half of the oracles of God" (the Old Testament), John reminded, "Yea and that half of which the Holy Ghost expressly declares that is 'profitable' as a means ordained by God for this very thing, 'for doctrine, for reproof, and instruction in righteousness'; to the end that 'the man of God may be prefect, thoroughly furnished unto all good works' [2 Tim. 3:16]." John made the same point when he described "the faith of Protestants," one of which he considered himself: "they believe neither more nor less than what is manifestly contained in, and provable by, the Holy Scriptures. The word of God is 'a lantern to their feet, and a light on all their paths.' . . . The written word is their whole and sole rule of faith, as well as practice."

While echoing the belief in *sola Scriptura* of the sixteenth-century Protestant Reformation, and taking the written Word as their own whole and sole rule of faith and practice, the Wesleys did not read Scripture in isolation from other spiritual resources. Both John and Charles were tried and true members of the Church of England, who resolved to live and die in the Church of England. Its Articles and Standard Homilies were embraced as authoritative summaries of biblical doctrine; its Prayer Book was (along with the Bible and the Methodist hymnbooks) their chief devotional aid. Charles, even more so than John, was determined to keep the Methodists from separating from the Church of England. Despite innovations like field preaching, itinerant evangelism, and lay preaching, John understood himself as nothing other than a loyal Anglican, who did not "defend or espouse any other principles to the best of my knowledge, than those which are plainly contained in the Bible, as well as in the Homilies and Book of Common Prayer." In his journal entry for September 13, 1739, John reported, "A serious clergyman desired to know in what points we [the Methodists] differed from the Church of England. I answered: 'To the best of my knowledge, in none. The doctrines we preach are the doctrines of the Church of England; indeed, the fundamental doctrines of the Church, clearly laid down, both in her Prayers, Articles, and Homilies.'"

The Primitive Church

As ardent Anglicans the Wesley brothers inherited an appreciation for the Christian tradition which was deepened and expanded by their own reading and experience in ministry. Both brothers were deeply enamored with the models of Christian doctrine and practice that came to them from "the primitive church." In his sermon "On Laying the Foundation of the New Chapel, near City-Road, London," John gave a sense of how he could discover the meaning of the "primitive church":

> This is the religion of the primitive Church, of the whole Church in the purist ages. It is clearly expressed, even in the small remains of Clemens Romanus, Ignatius, and Polycarp; it is even seen more at large in the writings of Tertullian, Origen, Clemens Alexandrinus, and Cyprian; and, even in the fourth century, it was found in the works of Chrysostom, Basil, Ephrem Syrus, and Marcarius.

This is a pretty heavy dose of readings from Christian antiquity for a person who purports to be "a man of one book"! Yet while Christian antiquity provided the norms and examples for Christian practice, Scripture alone was the main authority for Christian doctrine and practice. In his "Sermon on the Mount, XIII," John showed the interaction between Scripture and tradition as he placed his hope in "belonging to 'so excellent a church; reformed after the true Scripture model; blessed with the purest doctrine, the most primitive liturgy, the most apostolical form of government.'" In talking about the doctrine of sin, which was being taken lightly by some of his contemporaries, John insisted that "I do not know that ever it was controverted in the primitive Church." And then he added, in a flourish of Anglican triumphalism, "And here our own Church (as indeed in most points) exactly copies after the primitive."

In 1743, during a controversy with the Moravians over Christian practice, Charles wrote an extensive hymn entitled "Primitive Christianity," which was not only a study of the faith and practice of the early Christians but also an apology for Methodism — since in his view the Methodists were modern-day successors to that apostolic form and practice of Christian faith.

1. Happy the souls that first believed,
   To Jesus and each other cleaved:
   Join'd by the unction from above,
   In mystic fellowship of love.

2. Meek, simply followers of the Lamb,
   They lived, and spake, and thought the same!
   Brake the commemorative bread,
   And drank the Spirit of their Head.

3. On God they cast their every care,
   Wrestling with God in mighty prayer
   They claim'd the grace through Jesus given,
   By prayer they shut, and open'd heaven.

4. To Jesus they perform'd their vow,
   A little church in every house;
   They joyfully conspired to raise
   Their ceaseless sacrifice of praise.

While the Christian tradition offered models and examples for doctrine and practice, the definitive location of authority lay in Scripture alone. In a letter written in the midst of a disagreement with one William Dodd in March 1756, John expressed his fidelity to the Christian tradition while placing the authority of tradition under that of the Scriptures:

> In your last paragraph you say, "You set aside all authority, ancient and modern." Sir, who told you so? I never did; it never entered my thoughts. Who it was gave you that rule I know not; but my father gave it to me thirty years ago (I mean concerning reverence to the ancient Church and our own), and I have endeavoured to walk by it to this day. But I try every Church and every doctrine by the Bible. This is the word by which we are to be judged in that day.

The Case for Reason, Calmly Considered

John was an eminently rational person. In this character trait, John followed his mother, and was a marvel to his father, whereas emotionally mercurial Charles was more his father's child. Indeed, Samuel quipped to Susanna that even as a little boy "I think our Jack would not attend to the most pressing necessities of nature unless he could give a reason for it!" Writing, preaching, and ministering in the age of John Locke and common sense rationalism, the Wesley brothers had a deep appreciation for the religious role of enlightened human reason. In answering charges of enthusiasm and irrationality made by Rev. Dr. Rutherford, in an extensive letter of March 1768, John retorted, "You go on: 'It is a fundamental principle in the Methodist school that all who come into it must renounce their reason.' Sir, are you awake? Unless you are talking in your sleep, how can you utter so gross an untruth? It is a fundamental principle with us that to renounce reason is to renounce religion, that religion and reason go hand in hand, and that all irrational religion is false religion." In his Sermon No. 70, "The Case of Reason Impartially Considered," John continued this discussion by steering a middle course between those who "over-value reason" and those who "under-value reason." Hence, he wrote regarding the religious use of reason: "Why should you run from one extreme to the other? Is not the middle way best? Let reason do all reason can: Employ it as far as it will go. But, at the same time, acknowledge it is utterly incapable of giving either faith, or hope, or love; and consequently, of producing either real virtue or substantial happiness. Expect these from a higher source, even from the Father of the spirits of all flesh. Seek and receive them, not as you own acquisition, but as the gift of God." In this regard, Henry Rack rightly styles John Wesley as a "reasonable enthusiast," who combined the impulses of religious experience with a strong dose of common sense.

Experimental Divinity

After their conversion experiences in May 1738, the role of religious experience became vitally important to the Wesley brothers. They had learned that true Christianity was a religion that was able to be lived and felt. Indeed, both described the assurance that they received at their conversions with the language of feeling. John wrote: "I felt my heart was strangely warmed." His famous journal entry for May 24, 1738, reports that

> In the evening I went very unwillingly to a society in Aldersgate Street, where one was reading Luther's Preface to the Epistle to the Romans. About a quarter before nine, while he was describing the change which

God works in the heart through faith in Christ, I felt my heart strangely warmed. I felt I did trust in Christ, Christ alone for salvation, and an assurance was given me that he had taken away my sins, even mine, and saved me from the law of sin and death.

Three days earlier Charles had also "felt . . . a strange palpitation of heart," which he described more fully in one of the hymns he wrote over the next few days:

1. And can it be, that I should gain
   An interest in the Saviour's blood?
   Died He for me? — who caused His pain!
   For me? — who Him to death pursued.
   Amazing love! How can it be
   That Thou, my God, shouldst die for me? . . .

4. Long my imprison'd spirit lay,
   Fast bound in sin and nature's night:
   Thine eye diffused a quickening ray;
   I woke; the dungeon flamed with light;
   My chains fell off, my heart was free,
   I rose, went forth, and follow'd Thee.

5. Still the small inward voice I hear,
   That whispers all my sins forgiven;
   Still the atoning blood is near,
   That quench'd the wrath of hostile Heaven;
   I *feel* the life His wounds impart;
   I *feel* my Saviour in my heart.

When the Wesleys styled their 1780 standard Methodist hymnbook "a little body of experimental and practical divinity," they were giving voice to the role experience played in their theological reflection. True doctrine and true Christian practices should be able to be lived and experienced, and in that sense experience verifies and vivifies what is learned in Scripture and found illustrated in tradition. Thus John's sermons point to "the oracles of God and the testimony of their own experience" as a twin basis for accepting Christian doctrine or practice, but experience has a secondary role, with the primary role falling to Scripture. Hence, in defending the

Wesleyan doctrine regarding "the Witness of the Spirit," John wrote: " 'Experience is not sufficient to prove a doctrine which is not found in Scripture.' This is undoubtedly true, and it is an important truth. But this does not affect the present question, for it has been shown that this doctrine is founded on Scripture. Therefore experience is properly alleged to confirm it." Reason was also given this kind of secondary, confirming role. Indeed, Charles suggested that "proud" — and no doubt superficial — "learning" also meets its match when it comes to interpreting the saving, spiritual sense of "the sacred oracles":

> Proud learning boasts, its skill in vain
>   The sacred oracles to explain,
> It may the literal surface show,
>   But not the precious mine below;
> The saving sense remains conceal'd,
>   Till by the Spirit of faith reveal'd,
> The Book is still unread, unknown,
>   And open'd by the Lamb alone.

The Wesleyan Quadrilateral

Scott Jones's general conclusion is an apt one: "In Wesley's doctrine of authority, Scripture is given first place, but some role is also given to reason, Christian antiquity, experience and the Church of England." *The Book of Discipline of The United Methodist Church* seeks to clarify the relationship between resources in the following statement: "Wesley believed that the living core of the Christian faith was revealed in Scripture, illumined by tradition, vivified in personal experience, and confirmed by reason." The fourfold appeal to Scripture, tradition, reason, and experience has given rise to the "modern Methodist myth" of the so-called Methodist Quadrilateral. The imagery of a "Quadrilateral" has created a degree of ambiguity about the nature of Wesleyan doctrine in the United Methodist Church and in sister denominations. On the one hand, the adoption of the Quadrilateral metaphor for religious authority seemed to parallel a movement away from normative historical creeds and documents; on the other hand, as a four-sided geometric figure, the Quadrilateral seems to symbolize a quasi-equality between two parallel sides of the geometric figure. We have seen in the case of the Wesleys' own theology that this was not the case; there was no parallel authority that was equal to the authority of the Scriptures for them. Scripture, however, was read, confirmed, and applied in the life of the believer through the lens provided by attention to tradition, reason, and experience.

QUESTIONS FOR REVIEW

1. In what ways were the Wesleys heirs to the *sola Scriptura* doctrine of the Protestant Reformation? In what ways were they not?
2. How do you respond to the Wesleys' emphasis upon the Scriptures "as the only standard of truth, and only model of pure religion"?
3. What roles do you allow for Church tradition, reason, and experience when you explore religious ideas and practices?
4. What does it mean to say that reading the Scriptures is "a means of grace"? Do you think of the Scriptures in this way?
5. What do you think of the Wesleyan Quadrilateral? How would you describe the relative importance and relationship of those four resources of religious truth?

FOR FURTHER READING

Campbell, Ted. *John Wesley and Christian Antiquity* (Nashville: Abingdon/Kingswood, 1991).

Gunter, W. Stephen, et al. *Wesley and the Quadrilateral: Renewing the Conversation* (Nashville: Abingdon, 1997).

Jones, Scott. *John Wesley's Conception and Use of Scripture* (Nashville: Abingdon/Kingswood, 1995).

CHAPTER TWO

Purge the Foul Inbred Leprosy

....

SIN

> [The poor in spirit] has a deep sense of the loathsome leprosy of
> sin, which he brought with him from his mother's womb, which
> overspreads his whole soul, and totally corrupts every power and
> faculty thereof.
>
> John Wesley, Sermon No. 21

In his 1757 magnum opus *On the Doctrine of Sin* John Wesley gave that
theological doctrine a classical definition: "Sin is 'a transgression of the
law'; of that law of God to which a rational creature is subject.... As sin
involves the creature in guilt, that is, a liableness to punishment, the same
words are often used to denote either sin itself or guilt and punishment."
Few of John and Charles Wesley's doctrinal constructs evidence the impact of their theological context more than their treatment of sin, and in
particular original sin. They built their doctrine through their attention
to recurring biblical phrases like "in Adam all died," which pointed to the
extent of human sin ("all"), and the dire situation caused by it (spiritual
and physical "death"). Anchored in a direct affirmation of Scripture and
Christian tradition, their doctrine of sin was also, as John pointed out,
"confirmed by daily experience."

The Loathsome Leprosy

The Wesleys affirmed a doctrine of human depravity at a time when
enlightened people viewed it as a superstitious error that had debilitat-

16

ing effects upon human moral agency and action. While their sermons and hymns did not mount a direct attack upon the Deistic or Enlightenment understanding of human nature (though there are occasional asides), John's *Appeals* are another matter. They mount a direct assault upon ideas like the "innate moral virtue" of humans, and the essential (unspoiled) goodness of primitive human consciousness. In both cases, however, human depravity was the presupposition of the Wesleys' gospel of gracious restoration in an age that abounded with optimism about human nature and destiny. In a deft stroke, the Wesleys issued a challenge to the optimism of the age about *unaided* humanity as the appropriate basis for human moral action while co-opting its emphasis upon human dignity, moral action, and the ultimate perfectibility of humanity.

Seeking to curtail the Enlightenment's optimistic estimate of "natural man," the Wesleys pointed to human "sickness" or "sleepiness," which caused "the whole imaginations of the thoughts of [their] heart to be *only* evil . . . continually." Thus, John wrote, "we may learn one grand, fundamental difference between Christianity, considered as a system of doctrines, and the refined heathenism . . . they knew not men were empty of all good, and filled with all manner of evil." The fall of humanity that came from an abuse of human liberty made all — in their natural state — corrupt in their dispositions and liable to judgment. It turned people into active atheists or practical idolaters who traded the love of God for the love of the world, since they affixed to creation those loyalties they justly owed only to the Creator.

Pointing to contemporary accounts which stressed "the fair side of human nature" by depicting humanity as still being "a little lower than the angels" (Psalm 8:5), John was not surprised that these were "readily received by the generality of men. . . . For who is not easily persuaded to think favourably of himself? Accordingly writers of this kind are almost universally read, admired, applauded. . . . So that it is now quite unfashionable to talk otherwise, to say anything to the disparagement of human nature; which is generally allowed, notwithstanding a few infirmities, to be very innocent and wise and virtuous." "But in the meantime," John opined, "what must we do with our Bibles? For they will never agree with this. These accounts, however pleasing to flesh and blood, are utterly irreconcilable with the scriptural."

Using a mosaic of biblical phrases and images, John Wesley presented what he considered to be the biblical doctrine of original sin:

The Scripture avers that "by one man's disobedience all men were constituted sinners"; that "in Adam all died," spiritually died, lost the life and the image of God; that fallen, sinful Adam then "begat a son in his own likeness"; nor was it possible he should beget him in any other, for "who can bring a clean thing out of an unclean?" That consequently *we*, as well as other men, "were by nature" "dead in trespasses and sins," "without hope, without God in the world," and therefore "children of wrath"; that every man may say, "I was shapen in wickedness, and in sin did my mother conceive me"; that "there is no difference, in that all have sinned, and come short of the glory of God," of that glorious image of God wherein man was originally created.

John Wesley pointed out that Enlightenment optimists about human nature, while acknowledging that "*many* men are infected with many vices, and even born with a proneness to them . . . [nevertheless] suppose withal that in *some,* the natural goodness much over balances the evil." Yet the Scriptures, Wesley said, declare that "all men are conceived in sin . . . [and] 'all the imaginations of the thoughts of his heart [are] evil, *only* evil, and that continually.'" John concluded, "Hence . . . all who deny this — call it 'original sin' or by any other title — are but heathens still in the fundamental point which differences heathenism from Christianity." And in his extensive treatise on original sin John averred, "Either we must allow the imputation of Adam's sin, whatever difficulties attend to it, or renounce justification by Christ, and salvation through the merit of His blood." It was to this same theological effect that John reported a conversation he had with Lord Huntingdon, the Deistic son of his friend the Countess of Huntingdon, whose attitudes reflected too much the spirit of the English Enlightenment as represented by the teachings of David Hume, Lord Kames, and others:

If . . . [Lord Huntingdon declared] I was a sinner then I should need a Mediator. But I don't conceive I am. It is true, I often act wrongly for want of more understanding. And I frequently *feel* wrong tempers, particularly proneness to anger. But I cannot allow this to be a sin; for it depends on the motion of my blood and spirits, which I cannot help. Therefore, it cannot be a sin. Or if it be, the blame must fall on Him who made *me*.

As John Wesley would later write in his *magnum opus* on sin: "This is a fundamental truth; none will come to Christ as a Redeemer until he is thoroughly convinced he wants [needs] a Redeemer. No man will come to Him as a Savior till he knows and feels himself a lost sinner."

John took one last swipe at the empty optimism of his age and its human-centered understanding of salvation in a sermon he wrote less than a year before his death. "The Deceitfulness of the Human Heart" (Sermon No. 128) is based on Jeremiah 17:9, which proclaims: "The heart of man is deceitful above all things, and desperately wicked; who can know it?" Regarding the wickedness of the human heart, John concluded: "In considering this we have no need to refer to any particular sins (these are no more than the leaves, or at most the fruits, which spring from that evil tree), but rather the general root of all."

John and Charles Wesley's understanding of salvation as "the healing of souls" presupposes as universal the fatal disease that afflicts all humanity. Hence, in an early (1735) pre-conversion sermon, John described the world as one huge hospital ward: "The whole world is indeed, in its present state, only one great infirmary, all that are therein are sick of sin, and their one business there is to be healed." Sin is a great leveler of all human schemes of self-salvation, and the starting point for the Wesleys' conception of creation-wide salvation (justification and sanctification) by grace and faith. Indeed, four of the first five sermons in John Wesley's standard *Sermons on Several Occasions* give a discussion of original sin as a part of the preparation for the gospel. John Wesley could even suggest some benefits in the doctrine of original sin: "See then, you, upon the whole, how little reason we have to repine at the fall of our first parent, since herefrom we may derive such unspeakable advantages both in time and eternity."

A second important connection for the Wesleys' doctrine of sin, which was an obvious outgrowth of the first, was the structural role that sin played in their theology of salvation. The fall of the first Adam provides the pattern for redemption through the second Adam (Jesus Christ). Albert Outler described this as John's "dramatic theology of history"; it was foundational to Charles Wesley's understanding of salvation as well. Church fathers as ancient as Irenaeus (d. 198?) looked to the Pauline pairing of the first and second Adams to find a paradigm for speaking of humanity's long trek from being exiles of Eden to having the *imago Dei* (image of God) restored within them through the love of God and the work of God's Son. This pattern pervades the Wesleyan understanding of salvation, and gives Wesleyan theology a symmetry (John's word was "proportion") that they described as the "analogy of faith." It set the Wesleyan theology of salvation against the larger background of the plight of all humanity, and made the

Wesleys' theology of redemption less individualistic than the way we may have been accustomed to reading it. This approach gave the Wesleys a theology of history, in which "The Mystery of Iniquity" and "The Mystery of Godliness" are worked out on the broad stage of human events. And for all their criticism of the Enlightenment's view of human nature, the Wesleys embraced its optimism about the perfectibility of humanity — though only through God's grace — and thereby set their doctrine of original sin in a thoroughly constructive context. While coming "to the very edge of Calvinism"[1] in the way they ascribed the energy and impetus of salvation solely to God's grace, the Wesleys manifested an optimism about the availability of salvation to everyone that distinguished their view from Calvinism's narrower ("limited atonement") reading of the parameters of redemptive grace. Hence, on at least two separate occasions, John drew a direct line of connection from the fall of Adam to the redemption offered in Jesus Christ, setting both events in the context of divine, therapeutic grace. As John wrote: "if Adam had not fallen, Christ had not died."

Original Sin and Original Righteousness

John Wesley knew that the phrase "original sin" was the product of the ancient church of the fourth century; he traced it back to "either Chrysostom or Hilary," who used it to describe the text from Psalm 51:5: "Behold, I was conceived in iniquity, and in sin did my mother conceive me." Following Hilary's time, Wesley reported, St. Augustine and other writers brought the term into common use. As we saw above, the Wesleys did not insist on using the specific term "original sin," but they clearly believed that the doctrine of original sin was a biblical and foundational Christian teaching which must be affirmed — even in the face of spirited opposition.

The brothers had many euphemisms for original sin. The most common of these was "inbred sin," which clearly distinguished original sin, as a detrimental principle within all people, from sinful actions. Albert Outler amassed a lengthy list of references to "inbred sin" in John Wesley's sermons. The term is equally prominent in Charles's hymns:

1. In response to the query: "Wherein may we come to the very edge of Calvinism?" the Methodists replied: "1. In ascribing all good to the free grace of God. 2. In denying all natural free-will, all power antecedent to grace. And 3. In excluding all merit from man; even for what he has or does by the grace of God."

Show me, as my soul can bear
The depth of inbred sin,
All unbelief declare,
The pride that lurks within,
Take me, whom thyself has bought,
Bring into captivity
Every high aspiring thought
That would not stoop to Thee.

Charles often defined "inbred sin" as "pride that lurks within," as he did here. In other instances Charles described it as "the carnal mind":

Now my Joshua, bring me in!
Cast out my foes; the inbred sin,
The carnal mind remove;
The purchase of thy death divide;
And oh! With all the sanctified
Give me a lot of love.

John's journal describes "inbred sin" as "pride, anger, self-will, and un-belief." In his introduction to Sermon No. 44, "On Original Sin," Albert Outler reminds the reader that, for John, "in-being sin" was a synonym for "inbred sin" and "original sin"; he offered an example from 1766, in which John described his sermon "On Original Sin" as "that on In-Being Sin." Other Wesleyan metaphors for original sin included "sleep," in which one is "contented to remain in his fallen state, to live and die without the image of God" and "sickness," as in this hymn in which the singer prays:

Lord, I am sick; my sickness cure;
I want; do thou enrich the poor;
Under thy mighty hand I stoop:
O lift the abject sinner up!

A similar pattern emerged in Charles's sermon "Awake, Thou That Sleep-est," where the sinner, though "Full of diseases, as he is . . . fancies himself in perfect health. Fast bound in misery and iron, he dreams that he is happy and at liberty." When they come to name the disease that infects humanity, often the Wesleys describe it as "a deadly leprosy which they brought with them into the world." As Charles wrote,

21

A touch, a word, a look from thee
Can turn my heart, and make it clean;
Purge the foul inbred leprosy,
And save me from my bosom sin.

Seen in its destructive context, "my bosom sin" easily becomes one's "bosom foe," since both terms speak of sin as an enemy and destroyer lurking within the human breast. Similarly, original sin is frequently called "the root of bitterness" (Heb. 12:15) because of the way that it gives rise to the growth of all sorts of bitter fruit in a person's life. It is, as John described, "the evil root of a carnal mind" from which "stem evil tempers; pride and haughtiness of the spirit." Because of this, salvation, in the Wesleyan sense, must deal with both the "root" and the "branches" of sin in a person's life. As John wrote: "Thus you experience that he whose name is Jesus does not bear that name in vain; that he does in fact 'save his people from their sins'; the root as well as the branches." Hence, "by justification we are saved from the guilt of sin and restored to the favor of God: by sanctification we are saved from the power and root of sin, and restored to the image of God." Or as Charles put it in one of his hymns:

I right early shall awake
And see the Perfect Day;
Soon the Lamb of God shall take
My inbred-sin away;
When to me my Lord shall come,
Sin forever shall depart;
Jesus takes up all the room
In every believing heart.

John and Charles Wesley stressed that the original righteousness, in which humans had been created as bearing "the image of God" (Gen. 1:26), was the proper starting point for understanding full salvation — justification and sanctification — in human life. This is, as John wrote at length, the "great end of religion":

Ye know that the great end of religion is to renew our hearts in the image of God, to repair that total loss of righteousness and true holiness which we sustained by the sin of our first parent. Ye know that all religion which does not answer this end, all that stops short of this, the renewal of our soul in the image of God, after the likeness of him that created it, is not other than a poor farce and a mere mocking of God, to the destruction of our own soul.

Hence, as John wrote in his Sermon No. 5, "Justification by Faith": " 'In the Image of God was man made,' holy as he that created him is holy, merciful as the Author of all is merciful, perfect as his Father in heaven is perfect." Yet as he looked at the sinful world around him, it was easy for John to see that humans are "very far gone from original righteousness."

The Wesleyan sermon entitled "The One Thing Needful" is a prime example of the brothers' emphasis on original righteousness as the proper starting point for understanding redemption. Original sin, because of its interruption in this pattern, was a crucial doctrine for them because it described both the universal human need and humans' attempts to save themselves. But their goal in preaching redemption was larger than forgiveness for the guilt of sin — it was a transformation that also delivered persons from the *power* of sin.

"The One Thing Needful" was a sermon that John Wesley wrote during the brothers' American missionary adventure in Georgia. A note on the fly-leaf of the sermon says that Charles "transcribed from [John's] copies on board the *London Galley* between Charlestown and Boston, Sept. 1736." John may have written the sermon as early as 1734, and preached it (in some form or another) more than fifty times through 1790. Charles also valued the sermon very much and preached it several times, both before and after his conversion experience. Both brothers considered recovery of the "image of God" to be "the one thing needful" referenced in the sermon text (Luke 10:42). As they proclaimed in this sermon: "To recover our first estate, from which we are thus fallen, is the one thing now needful — to re-exchange the image of Satan for the image of God, bondage for freedom, sickness for health. Our one great business is to raise out of our souls the likeness of our destroyer, and to be born again, to be formed anew after the likeness of our Creator." Since love is both the image and the nature of God, an infusion of God's love is able to transform the human soul into its original, pristine state: "Love is the health of the soul," Wesley wrote, "the full exertion of all its power, the perfection of all its faculties. Therefore, since the enjoyment of these was the one end of our creation, the recovery of them is the one thing needful." As Charles prayed through one of his hymns:

23

Lord, if Thou wilt, I do believe,
Thou canst the saving grace impart;
Thou canst this instant forgive,
And stamp Thine image on my heart.

When this saving moment occurs, as John reported, "the deadly leprosy of sin, which they brought with them into the world, which no art of man could ever cure, is now clean departed from them."

A similar re-creation is envisioned for the entire sinful world, including inanimate creation, which has been subjected to "vanity" (Rom. 8:20) since Adam and Eve's fall. In one of his later sermons, "The New Creation" (1785), John Wesley envisioned a cosmic dimension to the restoration that was now occurring and one day would be made complete through the return of Jesus Christ. Preaching from the text, "Behold, I make all things new" (Rev. 21:5), Wesley opined that in the new, re-created heavens and earth, even natural disasters like floods, tornadoes, and earthquakes will be averted. But Wesley's redemptive concern was largely focused on humans. He looked forward to the day when "being returned both to the favor and image of God, thou shall know, love, and serve Him to all eternity. So that still the end of his life, the life of every man born into the world, is to know, love and serve his great Creator."

Sin "Properly So-called"

The emphasis John gave sin in his earliest sermons, especially those which stand on the shoulders of his popular evangelism, did not offer his famous distinction between sin "properly" and "improperly so-called." The early sermons stress original sin, and repeatedly link inner and outer sins, urging repentance and liberation from bondage to both types of sin. In fact, one of these sermons, the "Spirit of Bondage and Adoption," seems to go out of its way to argue that the issue of intentionality does not enter into the assessment of a person's guilt: "If thou doest [commit sin] is it willingly or unwillingly? In either case God hath told thee whose thou art — 'He that committeth sin is of the devil.'" Here John used the broadest conception of sin; in this sense Wesley followed the Protestant *sola fides* ("faith alone") tradition in emphasizing an understanding of human sin that undercuts all attempts at self-justification.

With this early foundation soundly in place, John Wesley turned his attention to the residual effects of sin in believers. In sermons like "The First Fruits of the Spirit" and "On Sin in Believers" he sought to clarify the connection between residual sin in believers and his understanding of sanctification as holy living. In "On Sin in Believers" he makes a distinction between willful transgression and "sins of infirmity" — including "involuntary failings" and "sins of surprise" — since "they that are in Christ and walk after the Spirit are not condemned . . . for anything whatever which they are not able to help." In a later section of the same sermon, Wesley sought to reconcile his understanding of salvation with this approach to human sin as well as that of other current theological expressions; here John criticized the Moravian notion that a person could be pure in heart but not in the "flesh" or physical life. John was willing to affirm the possibility of a believer's "sinlessness" with respect to outward sin, but he could not agree that a believer, as soon as she/he is justified, is "freed from all sin." Hence, Wesley concluded, "although even babies in Christ are *sanctified,* yet it is only *in part.* . . . Accordingly, believers are continually exhorted to watch against the flesh, as well as the world, and the devil." This means that believers, while forgiven and being transformed by justification and new birth, are not a finished work with respect to freedom from the power of sin.

This line of development in John Wesley's doctrine of sin reached its apex in his sermon entitled "The Great Privilege of Those that Are Born of God" (Sermon No. 19). Here John defines sin "according to the plain, common acceptation of the word: an actual, voluntary 'transgression of the law'; of the revealed, written law of God; of any commandment of God acknowledged to be such at the time it is transgressed." This emphasis upon "voluntary transgression" signals a shift away from the emphasis on original guilt and toward a stress upon actual, willful sins as the basis of our condemnation before God. This shift was not due to any change in Wesley's understanding of the depth of human sinfulness. Randy Maddox put it this way: "Wesley's growing uncomfortableness with the notion of inherited guilt was not due to any doubt about universal human sinfulness, but rather was an expression of his life-long conviction that God deals reasonably with each individual. This conviction led him to locate the issue of guilt in our own sins rather than the sins of our ancestors. More broadly it inclined him to focus less on the origin of sins than on the fact of sin's present infection of our own nature (and our resulting need for God's grace)."

A second factor in the development of John's doctrine of "sin properly so-called" is the emergence of the Wesleyan doctrine of Christian Perfection as a remedy for human sin. If one looks at sin as everything that "falls short of the glory of God," then it is clear that there is no such thing as Christian Perfection in this life. But if one is willing to focus one's attention upon sins that are acknowledged, voluntary, and willful, then a deliverance from this sort of sin might be conceivable through the utter transformation of a person's mind, soul, and will. Hence, as Colin Williams pointed out: "It is clear that Wesley's view of Perfection depends upon a distinction between two kinds of sin. In terms of sin in the absolute sense, as measured by the 'perfect law,' there is no such thing as perfection in believers. In terms of sin as conscious separation from Christ there can be found perfection — a perfection of an unbroken conscious dependence upon Christ."

While there is no direct evidence that Charles Wesley followed John in this voluntarist and willful definition of sin "properly so-called," it is clear that he followed John's later emphasis upon "sins" as well as "sin" as a principle within. Charles seems to have maintained an unqualified conception of sin, and a correspondingly unqualified conception of Christian Perfection, as we will see later. His approach is evident in a stanza from his famous hymn on Christian Perfection, "Love Divine, All Loves Excelling." Perhaps thinking this verse was too apt to be misunderstood because of its reference to "our power of sinning," John omitted it from their standard hymn book. This stanza, in Charles's original lyrics, prays for a redemption that means a deliverance from "sins" — as well as from the very power that causes sins in human life:

> Breathe, O breathe Thy loving Spirit
> Into every troubled breast,
> Let us all in Thee inherit,
> Let us find that second rest;
> Take away our *power* of sinning,
> Alpha and Omega be,
> End of faith as its beginning,
> Set our hearts at liberty.[2]

2. This verse is often altered to read, in line five: "Take away our bent to sinning." But Charles's original lyrics are as quoted here. The reference to the "beginning" here may be a nod towards original righteousness.

QUESTIONS FOR FURTHER REFLECTION

1. How do you think of human sin?
2. What role do you see sin playing in the process of salvation?
3. Are you able to distinguish between sin (as principle within) and sins which people sometimes commit?
4. What do you think about John Wesley's definition of "sin in believers" as "a voluntary transgression of a known law of God"?

SUGGESTIONS FOR FURTHER READING

Maddox, Randy. *Responsible Grace* (Nashville: Kingswood/Abingdon, 1994), pp. 73-83.
Wesley, John. *The Doctrine of Original Sin.*
Wesley, John. Sermon No. 19, "The Great Privilege of Those Born of God."

CHAPTER THREE

My Chains Fell Off

THE NEW BIRTH

My chains fell off/My heart was free. . . .

"Free Grace," Charles Wesley, 1738

Looking back upon his Oxford years, as the "Holy Club" was coming together, John Wesley wrote, "A year or two after 1726, Mr. Law's *Christian Perfection* and *Serious Call* were put into my hands. These convinced me, more than ever, of the absolute impossibility of being half a Christian; and I determined, through His grace . . . to be all devoted to God, to give Him my soul, my body and my substance." Charles Wesley, whose journal is silent about the Oxford years, reported having his own spiritual awakening during this same period in an autobiographical letter:

> My first year at College I was lost in diversions. The next I set myself to study. Diligence led me into serious thinking. I went to the weekly sacrament, and persuaded two or three young scholars to accompany me, and to observe the method of study prescribed by the statutes of the University. This gained me the harmless nickname of a Methodist. . . . We then proceeded regularly in our studies, and in doing what good we could to the bodies and souls of men.

In the Oxford "Holy Club," the Wesley brothers joined with several friends, including the future fiery evangelist George Whitefield, "in doing what good we could to the bodies and souls of men." They were diligently seeking after that "holiness without which no one shall see God" (Heb. 12:14). The Oxford Methodists practiced spiritual disciplines like corporate and private prayer, Bible study, fasting, alms giving, and prison visitation. They were earnest young men who sought to live holy lives unto God, and thereby gain God's acceptance.

"Almost a Christian"

John Wesley described his state of soul during this period, in his 1741 Oxford sermon, "The Almost Christian." It was based on Acts 26:28, and preached in St. Mary's church, before the assembled university. Speaking autobiographically about his earlier life at Oxford, John declared:

> I did go thus far for many years, as many of this place can testify; using diligence to eschew all evil, and to have a conscience void of offence; redeeming the time, buying up every opportunity of doing all good to all men; constantly and carefully using all the public and all the private means of grace; endeavouring after a steady seriousness of behaviour at all times and in all places. And God is my record, before whom I stand, doing all this in sincerity; having a real design to serve God, a hearty desire to do his will in all things, to please him who had called me "to fight the good fight," and to "lay hold of eternal life." Yet my own conscience beareth me witness in the Holy Ghost that all this time I was but "almost a Christian."

It was in this same frame of mind that John, Charles, and two of their Oxford colleagues went to Georgia on a missionary adventure sponsored by the Anglican Society for the Propagation of the Gospel, in 1735-36. John's journal entry for October 14, 1735, described their frame of mind in undertaking that work: "Our end in leaving our native country was not to avoid want (God having given us plenty of temporal blessings), nor to obtain the dung or dross of riches or honor; but singularly this — to save our souls, to live wholly to the glory of God."

The Wesleys were — using John's famous "threefold states of man" — "legal" men, who had been awakened by God from the slumber of sin and thoughtlessness before God ("natural man"), and who sought to earn their salvation by good works and keeping the whole law of God. "Legal man" is an inveterate do-gooder; he seems to be — from all external appearances — a good Christian. But "legal man" lives his life under a terrible bondage of duty in trying to keep the whole law of God, and of failure and despair because no one — unaided by God's grace — can keep God's law perfectly. Hence, John wrote: "How low a portraiture is this one 'under the law'! One who feels the burden he cannot shake off; who pants after liberty, power and love, but is in fear and bondage still! Until that time that God answers the wretched man crying out, 'Who will deliver me from this bondage of sin, from this body of death?'"

En route to and on the American continent the Wesleys met German Moravian missionaries — distant theological descendents of Martin Luther — who tried (to no avail) to witness to them about justification by faith. Soon after he arrived in Georgia, John had a soul-searching conversation with August Spangenburg, one of the pastors among the Moravians. Wesley asked Spangenburg's advice about his own spiritual pilgrimage, and he told John, "My brother, I must first ask you one or two questions. Have you the witness within yourself? Does the Spirit of God bear witness with your spirit that you are a child of God?" Wesley reported in his journal, "I was surprised, and knew not what to answer. He observed it, and asked, 'Do you know Jesus Christ?' I paused, and said, 'I know he is the Saviour of the world.' True, replied he, 'but do you know he has saved *you?*' I answered, 'I hope he has died to save me.' He only added, "Do you know yourself?' I said, 'I do.' But I fear they were vain words." Looking back over his Georgia experience, John later described it this way: "I went to America to convert the Indians, but oh! Who will convert me? Who, what is he that will deliver me from this evil heart of unbelief? I have a fair summer religion. I can talk well; nay, and believe myself, while no danger is near: but let death look me in the face, and my spirit is troubled."

Justification by Faith Alone

From the distance of May 24, 1738, John described his preaching ministry in Savannah as "beating the air." "Being ignorant of the righteousness of Christ, which by a living faith in him bringeth salvation 'to every one that believeth,'" John wrote, "I sought to establish my own righteousness, and so laboured in the fire all my days." Back in England, in the spring of 1738, the Wesleys ministered as they were able and began to converse with Peter Böhler, a second Moravian missionary. On Saturday, February 4, John reported, "I found my brother [Charles] at Oxford, recovering from his pleurisy; and with him Peter Böhler. By whom (in the hand of the great God) I was on Sunday the 5th clearly convinced of unbelief, of the want ["lack"] of 'that faith whereby alone we are saved [Acts 4:12],' with the full, Christian salvation." About six weeks later, John met again with Peter Böhler:

> Sat. 22 [March] I met Peter Böhler once more. I had now no objection to what he said of the nature of faith, viz. that it is (to use the words of our Church), "A sure trust and confidence which a man hath in God, that through the merits of Christ *his* sins are forgiven, and *he* reconciled to the favour of God." Neither could I deny either the happiness or holiness which he described as fruits of this living faith.

Meanwhile, Charles was preaching and battling the illnesses he had contracted in Georgia — chiefly pleurisy. During his convalescence, he too had been in conversation with Moravian missionaries. On February 18, 1738, Charles first met Peter Böhler, and six days later they had a soul-searching conversation about saving faith when the Moravian came to visit him while Wesley lay upon his sickbed. Böhler asked Charles, "Do you hope to be saved?" Charles replied: "Yes." Peter pressed him, "For what reason do you hope it?" Charles said: " 'Because I have used my best endeavours to serve God.' He [Böhler] shook his head, and said no more. I thought him very uncharitable, saying in my heart, 'What, are not my endeavours a sufficient ground of hope? Would he rob me of my endeavours? I have nothing else to trust to.' " On May 6, Charles confided in his journal: "God still kept up the little spark of desire which he himself had enkindled in me, and I seemed determined to speak of, and wish for, nothing but faith in Christ. Yet could not this preserve me from sin, which I this day ran into with my eyes open. So that after ten years' vain struggling, I own and feel it absolutely unconquerable."

Both Charles and John had a long-distance encounter with Martin Luther, the ardent advocate for justification by faith, during the month of May 1738. Charles's journal entry for May 17 reported, "Today I first saw Luther on the Galatians, which Mr. [William] Holland had accidentally lit upon. We began [reading him], and found him nobly full of faith." Later that same evening, Charles Wesley confided, "I spent some hours this evening in private with Martin Luther, who was greatly blessed to me, especially his conclusion of the second chapter. I laboured, waited, and prayed to see 'who loved *me* and gave himself for *me*' [Gal. 1:6-7]. When nature near exhausted forced me to bed, I opened the book upon 'For he will finish the work, and cut it short in righteousness, because a short work will the

Lord make upon earth' [Rom. 9:28]. After this comfortable assurance that he [Christ] would come, and would not tarry, I slept in peace."

Five days later, on the day of Pentecost, Mrs. Musgrave, one of Charles's nurses, challenged him with the words, "In the name of Jesus of Nazareth, arise, believe, and thou shalt be healed of thy infirmities!" Charles "[l]ay musing and trembling," he later recalled, "then thought, 'but what if it should be him!'" Daring to risk faith in Christ, Charles "felt a strange palpitation of heart. I said, yet feared to say, 'I believe, I believe!'" His newfound faith was confirmed by opening the Psalter to a providentially appropriate verse: "Blessed is the man whose unrighteousness is forgiven, and whose sin is covered. Blessed is the man to whom the Lord imputeth no sin and in whose spirit is no guile" [Psalm 32:2, Book of Common Prayer].

The next day Charles wrote, "I now found myself at peace with Christ and rejoiced in the hope of loving Christ. My temper for the rest of the day was mistrust of my own great, but before unknown, weakness. I saw that by faith I stood; by the continual support of faith, which kept me from falling, though of myself I am ever sinking into sin. I went to bed still sensible of my own weakness (I humbly hope to be more and more so), yet confident of Christ's protection." Then two days later, "I waked under the protection of Christ, and gave myself up, soul and body, to him. At nine I began [writing] a hymn upon my conversion."

Meanwhile, across town, John Wesley was on the verge of his own encounter with Christ through the words of Martin Luther. He had still another soul-searching conversation with Peter Böhler about the nature of saving faith, and this time the Moravian brought with him three witnesses who "testified of their own personal experience that a true living faith in Christ is inseparable from a sense of pardon for all past, and freedom from all present sins. They added with one mouth that this faith was the gift, the free gift of God, and that he would surely bestow it upon every soul who earnestly and perseveringly sought it." John "resolved to seek it to the end (1) by absolutely renouncing all dependence . . . upon *my own* works or righteousness, on which I had really grounded my hope of salvation, though I knew it not, from my youth up; (2) by adding to 'the constant use of all the' other 'means of grace,' continual prayer for this very thing, justifying, saving faith, a full reliance on the blood of Christ shed for *me;* a trust in him as *my* Christ, as *my* sole justification, sanctification, and redemption."

On May 24, 1738, after spending the day in prayer, worship, and Scripture study, John described in his journal his activities in these famous words: "In the evening I went very unwillingly to a society in Aldersgate Street, where one was reading Luther's Preface to the Epistle to the Romans. About a quarter before nine, while he was describing the change which God works in the heart through faith in Christ, I felt my heart strangely warmed. I felt I did trust in Christ, Christ alone for salvation, and an assurance was given me that he had taken away *my* sins, even *mine,* and saved *me* from the law of sin and death."

Charles Wesley's journal picks up John's story at this point: "Towards ten my brother was brought in triumph by a troop of our friends and declared, 'I believe.' We sang the hymn with great joy, and parted with prayer." Exactly *which* Charles Welsey conversion hymn "To Christ" was sung on this occasion is a matter of some debate. Among the possible choices, "And Can It Be," which Charles entitled "Free Grace," is the most famous. It strikes an autobiographical note that resonated with the conversion experiences of both brothers:

3. He left His Father's throne above,
     (So free, so infinite His grace!)
   Emptied Himself of all but love,
     And bled for *Adam's* helpless race;
   'Tis mercy all, immense and free!
   For, O my God! It found out me!

4. Long my imprison'd spirit lay,
     Fast bound in sin and nature's night:
   Thine eye diffused a quickening ray;
     I woke; the dungeon flamed with light;
   My chains fell off, my heart was free,
   I rose, went forth, and follow'd Thee.

5. Still the small inward voice I hear,
     That whispers all my sins forgiven;
   Still the atoning blood is near,
     That quench'd the wrath of hostile Heaven:
   I feel the life His wounds impart;
   I feel my Saviour in my heart.

6. No condemnation now I dread,
     Jesus, and all in Him, is mine;

Alive in Him, my Living Head,
  And clothed in righteousness Divine,
Bold I approach th'eternal throne,
And claim the crown, through Christ, my own.

The Standing Topic

Four days after his Aldersgate experience John Wesley preached a sermon at Long Acre Chapel, in London, from the text of Romans 4:5, "To him that worketh not, but believeth on him, that justifieth the ungodly, his faith is counted to him for righteousness." A sermon on that same text was subsequently published under the title "Justification by Faith." What did John mean by justification? "The plain scriptural notion of justification is pardon, the forgiveness of sins. It is that act of God the Father whereby, for the sake of the propitiation made by the blood of his Son, he 'showeth forth his righteousness (or mercy) by the remission of sins that are past.'" In a subsequent sermon, John added, "Justification is another word for pardon. It is the forgiveness of all our sins, and (what is necessarily implied therein) our acceptance with God."

With his usual clarity John Wesley distinguished justification from sanctification by stressing that the former is what God does *for us* in Jesus Christ, whereas the latter is what God does *in* us through the work of the Spirit of Christ:

> . . . it is evident from what has been already observed that [justification] is not the being made actually just and righteous. This is *sanctification;* which is indeed in some degree the immediate *fruit* of justification, but nevertheless is a distinct gift of God, and of a totally different nature. The one implies what God *does for us* through his Son; the other what he *works in us* by his Spirit.

In May and June of 1738, Charles continued to recover from his illness and began to witness to his friends and family about the reality of salvation by faith. On Sunday, July 2, he wrote in his journal: "Being to preach this morning for the first time [since his conversion], received strength for the work of the ministry in prayer and singing. . . . I preached 'Salvation by Faith' to a deeply attentive audience. Gave the cup. Observing a woman full of reverence, I asked her if she had forgiveness of sins. She answered, with great sweetness and humility, 'Yes, I know it now that I have forgiveness.'" Preaching at "London Wall," a second time that same afternoon, "without fear or weariness," Charles was stopped by a woman as he entered the church, who "blessed me most heartily, telling me she had received forgiveness of sins while I was preaching in the morning."

John's preaching ministry was taking a similar track. On June 11th he was scheduled to preach at St. Mary's, Oxford, and he did — from the text of Ephesians 2:8, "By grace ye are saved through faith." The sermon was entitled "Salvation by Faith," and it stands as No. 1, in his *Sermons on Several Occasions,* as a manifesto of the new direction his ministry was taking. A three point sermon, "Salvation by Faith" inquired "(1) What faith it is through which we are saved. (2) What is the salvation which is through faith. And (3) How we are to answer some objections."

After exploring what saving faith is *not,* John summarized saving faith:

It acknowledges his [Christ's] death as the only sufficient means of redeeming man from death eternal, and his resurrection as the restoration of us all to life and immortality; inasmuch as he "was delivered for our sins, and rose again for our justification." Christian faith is then not only an assent to the whole gospel of Christ, but also a full reliance on the blood of Christ, a trust in the merits of his life, death and resurrection; a recumbency upon him as our atonement and our life, as *given for us,* and *living in us.* It is a sure confidence which a man hath in God, that through the merits of Christ *his* sins are forgiven, and *he* reconciled to the favour of God; and in consequence hereof a closing with him and cleaving to him as our "wisdom, righteousness, sanctification, and redemption," or in one word, our salvation.

Asking what is it from which a person is "saved," John proclaimed: "Ye are saved (to comprise all in one word) from sin." Hence, " 'he will save his people from their sins': from original and actual, past and present sin, of the flesh and of the spirit. Through faith that is in him they are saved both from the guilt and from the power of sin." Wesley explained this salvation:

This then is the salvation which is through faith, even in the present world: a salvation from sin and the consequences of sin, both often expressed in the word "justification," which taken in the largest sense, implies a deliverance from guilt and punishment, by the atonement of Christ actually applied to the soul of the sinner now believing on him, and a deliverance from the power of sin, through Christ "formed in his heart." So that he who is thus justified or saved by faith is indeed "born again." He is "born again of the Spirit" unto a new "life which is hid with Christ in God."

By September Charles was well again and preaching all over London. His terse journal entry for Sunday, September 3rd, for example, reports: "Preached Salvation by Faith at Westminster Abbey; gave the cup. In the afternoon preached at St. Botolph. Expounded Rom. 2 at Syms's, to above two hundred people." It has been suggested that Charles may have used John's university sermon at Westminster Abbey; whether or not that is true, the replication of the title and subject matter of the sermon indicates that he and John were on the same page with respect to this foundational doctrine. The sermon that Charles preached the same day, at St. Botolph's, was (according to his sermon register) based on 1 John 3:14, "We know that we have passed from death unto life." Charles preached the first part of the sermon that day; it stresses the "three states of man" and the new life that is ours through faith in Christ. Charles concluded: "I trust there is more than one here present who finds that he hath laid hold of the hope set before him, that believing he hath everlasting life and rejoices in God through our Lord Jesus Christ by whom he hath now received the atonement, the Spirit also bearing witness with his own spirit that he is a child of God."

Charles's subsequent sermon on Romans 3:23-24, which he wrote and preached the next spring, addressed the topic of justification by faith even more directly:

> . . . justification is the office of God only, and is not a thing which we render unto him, but which we receive of him. By his free mercy, and by the only merits of his most dearly beloved Son, our only Redeemer, Saviour, and Justifier, Jesus Christ.

On July 1, 1739, Charles also preached justification by faith "before the university with great boldness. All were very attentive. One could not help weeping." Charles's text was Romans 3:23-25: "All have sinned and come short of the glory of God, being justified freely by his grace, through the redemption that is in Jesus Christ; whom God hath set forth to be a propitiation through faith in his blood." He insisted that this was no new doctrine, having been well established in the Scriptures and the teachings of the

Church of England: "Let not those therefore who deny this doctrine any longer call themselves of the Church of England. They may be of the Church of Rome, but cannot be of ours, who allow works any share in our justification with God. Papists indeed they are, though they may not know it."

In his *Short History of Methodism* (1781), John Wesley described this period in the history of the movement: "they began to be convinced that 'by grace we are saved through faith'; that justification by faith was the doctrine of the Church, as well as the Bible. As soon as they believed, they spake; salvation by faith being now their standing topic." He wrote that justification by faith "implied three things: (1) That men are all, by nature, 'dead in sin,' and consequently 'children of wrath.' (2) That they are 'justified by faith alone.' (3) That faith produces inward and outward holiness: And these points," he recalled, "they insisted on day and night. In a short time they became popular preachers. The congregations were large wherever they preached. The former name was then revived; and all these gentlemen, with their followers, were entitled Methodists."

The New Birth

The Wesleys considered the New Birth, along with justification by faith, to be among the fundamental doctrines of the Christian faith. These two doctrines are deeply interrelated; as soon as a person is justified ("pardoned" or "forgiven"), that person experiences the New Birth. These two aspects are so closely related that they are frequently confused. As John explained:

> It has been frequently supposed that the New Birth and justification were only different expressions describing the same thing; it being certain on the one hand that whoever is justified is also born of God, and on the other [hand] that whoever is born of God is also justified; yet that both these gifts of God are given to every believer in one and the same moment. In one point in time his sins are blotted out and he is born of God.

Hence, the New Birth is said to immediately accompany justification: "We allow that at the very moment of justification we are 'born again,' in that instant we experience that inward change from darkness into marvelous light, from the image of the brute and the devil, into the image of God, from the earthly, sensual, devilish mind, to the mind which was in Christ

Jesus." So the New Birth is the beginning of sanctification, and is sometimes called "Initial Sanctification" because it begins that long process whereby a person is wholly renewed by faith in Christ and the work of the Holy Spirit within. As John explained:

> . . . at the same time that we are justified, yea, in that very moment, *sanctification* begins. In that instant we are "born again," "born from above," "born of the Spirit." There is a *real* as well as a *relative* change. We are inwardly renewed by the power of God. We feel the "love of God shed abroad in our heart by the Holy Ghost which is given to us," producing love to all mankind and more especially to the children of God; expelling the love of the world, the love of pleasure, of ease, of honour, of money, together with pride, anger, self-will, and every other evil temper — in a word, changing the "earthly sensual devilish" into the mind that was in Christ Jesus.

In our order of thinking, justification by faith precedes the New Birth, but in actuality they happen at the same time: "in the moment we are justified by the grace of God through the redemption that is in Jesus we are also 'born of the Spirit,' but in order of thinking, as it is termed, justification precedes the New Birth. We first conceived his wrath to be turned away, and [then] his Spirit to work in our heart." In another place John wrote: "Justification implies only a relative, the New Birth a real, change. God in justifying us does something *for* us; in begetting us again he does the work *in* us. The former changes our outward relation to God . . . by the latter our inmost souls are changed, so that . . . we become saints. The one restores us to the favor [of God], the other to the image of God." Charles Wesley's hymn based on John 3:7, "Marvel not that I said unto thee, ye must be born again," communicates this same emphasis upon spiritual renewal and restoration:

1. Adam descended from above
     Thou only canst that Spirit impart,
   That principle of heavenly love
     Regenerating the sinful heart:
   O might He now from Thee proceed,
     Fountain of life and purity,
   Implant the nature of our Head,
     And work the mighty change in me.

2. The seed infused, the good desire,
   Into a tree immortal raise,
With all Thy sanctity inspire,
   With all Thy plenitude of grace;
Spotless, and spiritual and good,
   My heart and life shall be Thine,
And in my Lord's similitude
   Renew'd I shall for ever shine.

The Wesleys continued their contact with William Law during the early years of the revival. John wrote him several letters, acknowledging that he "was once a kind of oracle to me." Charles visited William Law on August 10, 1739, and as they took up "the standing topic" Charles confessed that he had been, before Whitsunday 1738, confused about the difference between justification and sanctification. He implied that Law's books and teaching were part of the reason for that confusion: "I told him, he was my schoolmaster to bring me to Christ; but the reason why I did not come sooner to Him, was, my seeking to be sanctified before I was justified."

By the next spring, both brothers were being excluded from the London churches for preaching justification by faith. In his *A Farther Appeal to Men of Reason and Religion* (1745), John explained this situation. As soon as they had discovered justification by faith, the brothers made it their standing topic wherever they preached. Initially they were overwhelmed by invitations to serve as guest preachers, but soon the requests for their services dried up, and they were forbidden to preach in churches where they had previously been welcomed. "Things were in this posture," John wrote, "when I was told I must preach no more in this, and this, and another church; the reason was usually added without reserve, 'Because you preach such doctrines.'" "Be pleased to observe," John continued, "that I was forbidden, as general consent, to preach in any church (though not by any judicial sentence), 'for preaching such doctrine.' This was the open, avowed cause; there was at the same time no other, either real or pretended, except that the people crowded so."

Excluded from the churches, John and Charles Wesley followed George Whitefield into the scandalous innovation of "field preaching." Preaching alfresco took the Wesleys to where the unchurched, needy people were. Now they had both their new message and a new method for communicating it. The Wesleyan revival had begun.

QUESTIONS FOR REFLECTION

1. What does "justification by faith" mean to you?
2. What does "the New Birth" mean to you?
3. What did John Wesley mean when he described himself and others as "almost a Christian"?
4. What is "the standing topic" of your Christian life?
5. Have you ever had a Christian experience that made you feel "free"?

SUGGESTIONS FOR FURTHER READING

Cannon, William R. *John Wesley's Theology, With Special Reference to the Doctrine of Justification* (Nashville: Abingdon Press, 1946).

Rattenbury, J. Ernest. *The Evangelical Doctrines of Charles Wesley's Hymns* (London: Epworth Press, 1942), chapters 14-15.

Wesley, Charles. Sermon No. 3, "Awake, Thou That Sleepest."

———. "And Can It Be."

Wesley, John. Sermon No. 1, "Salvation by Faith."

———. Sermon No. 5, "Justification by Faith."

———. Sermon No. 45, "The New Birth."

CHAPTER FOUR

Pure and Spotless Let Us Be

HOLINESS

Question: What may we reasonably believe to be God's design in raising up preachers called Methodists? Answer: Not to form a new Sect, but to reform the nation, particularly the church, and to spread *Scriptural holiness* over the land.

John Wesley, Sermon No. 107

As we have observed in chapter 3, the Wesley brothers distinguished between justification and sanctification as two separate events of God's grace, and yet closely linked justification and sanctification by describing them as intimately interrelated experiences. They saw justification as "pardon," what God does *for us* through faith in Jesus Christ, whereas sanctification was a "real change" which God begins to work *in us* by the power of the Holy Spirit because of our faith in Jesus Christ. As John wrote in "Working Out Our Own Salvation," based on Philippians 2:12-13, "By justification we are saved from the guilt of sin, and restored to the favor of God; by sanctification we are saved from the power and root of sin, and restored to the image of God."

This distinction between justification and sanctification was important to the Wesley brothers because of the trials of their own spiritual pilgrimage, the painful years that they had spent seeking "the holiness without which no one shall see God" before they had experienced God's justifying grace. The frustration and spiritual anguish that the Wesleys experienced in those early years of striving as "almost Christians" and "legal men" caused them to distinguish between justification and sanctification and put those events in the proper sequence: first a person is justified by faith, then sanctification begins. Whereas justification was a state of having God's acceptance, sanctification described a process of being made holy within by the work of the Holy Spirit. Sanctification, hence, was viewed both as a separate and distinct gift of God, and as being the immediate fruit of justification.

The Wesleys both stressed the logical and theological difference between justification and sanctification, as well as their spiritual and experiential unity. Taken together, justification and sanctification comprise the whole of Christian salvation. And, as John reported, "All experience, as well as Scripture, shows this salvation to be both instantaneous and gradual. It begins the moment we are justified, in the holy, humble, gentle, patient love of God and man. It gradually increases from that moment, as a 'grain of mustard seed, which at first is the least of all seeds, but' gradually 'puts forth large branches,' and becomes a great tree; till in another instant the heart is cleansed from all sin, and filled with pure love to God and man. But even that love increases more and more, till we 'grow up in all things into him that is our head,' till we 'attain the measure and stature of the fullness of Christ.'" Thus, justification occurs in an instant. It precedes and begins the process of sanctification. Sanctification is a long process punctuated by moments of experiential transition, the first of which is called "New Birth," and the last of which is called "Entire Sanctification" or "Christian Perfection."

The theological and experiential bridge between justification and sanctification is the New Birth. The New Birth is sometimes called "Initial Sanctification" because it begins the work of God within the newly justified Christian. Justification and New Birth are, as John Wesley described them, distinct yet inseparable:

> But though it be allowed that justification and the New Birth are in point of time inseparable from each other, yet they are easily distinguished as being not the same, but things of a widely distinct nature. Justification implies only a relative, the New Birth a real, change. God in justifying us does something *for* us; in begetting us again he does the work *in* us. The former changes our outward relation to God, so that of enemies we become children; by the latter our inmost souls are changed; so that of sinners we become saints. The one restores us to the favor, the other to the image of God. The one taking away the guilt, the other taking away the power, of sin. So that although they are joined together in time, yet are they of widely distinct natures.

John made many of these same points in sermon No. 19, "The Scripture Way of Salvation," in which he wrote: "At the same time that we are justified, yea, in that very moment, *sanctification* begins. In that instant we are 'born again,' 'born from above,' 'born of the Spirit.'" Once again John described the New Birth and the sanctification which it begins in terms of the "*real* and *relative* change" which God works in believers through the power of the Holy Spirit. This change is "real" in that the person is actually being inwardly renewed by the power of God, and it is a "relative change" insofar as it is the kind of change that keeps on happening until the process is entirely complete. As John put it, "we are inwardly renewed by the power of God. We feel the 'love of God shed abroad in our heart by the Holy Ghost which is given unto us,' by producing love to all mankind and more especially to the children of God; expelling the love of the world, the love of pleasure, of ease, of honor, of money; together with pride, anger, self-will and every other evil temper — in a word, changing the 'earthly, sensual, devilish mind' into 'the mind which was in Christ Jesus.'" Hence, "From the time of our being 'born again' the gradual work of sanctification takes place." This process involves the removal of the fallen nature and its fruits, so that the Christian becomes more and more Christlike. Hence, in "On God's Vineyard," John described the New Birth as "the gate" or beginning of the process of sanctification: "the same time a man is justified sanctification properly begins. For when he is justified he is 'born again,' 'born from above,' 'born of the spirit.' Which although it is not (as some suppose) the whole process of sanctification, [it] is doubtless the gate of it."

Holiness without Which No One Shall See God

In John's sermon on "The New Birth" he gave an extensive reply to the question: "what is holiness according to the oracles of God?" In typical form, he began by describing what true scriptural holiness is *not:* "Not a bare external religion, a round of outward duties, how many soever they be, and how exactly soever performed. No; gospel holiness is no less than the image of God stamped upon the heart." And then, also characteristically, John went on at great length to describe this holiness by stringing together biblical phrases and allusions:

It is no other than the whole mind which was in Christ Jesus. It consists of all heavenly affections and tempers mingled together in one. It implies such a continual, thankful love to him who hath not withheld from us his Son, his only Son, as makes it natural, and in a manner necessary to us, to love every child of man; as fills us with "bowels of mercies, kindness, gentleness, long-suffering." It is such a love of God as teaches us to be blameless in all manner of conversation; as enables us to present our souls and bodies, all we are and all we have, all our thoughts, words, and actions, [as] a continual sacrifice to God, acceptable through Christ Jesus.

It is notable that "faith is the condition of sanctification exactly as it is of justification. It is the condition: none is sanctified but he that believes; without faith no man is sanctified. And it is the only condition: this alone is sufficient for sanctification." This means, contrary to John and Charles's earlier way of thinking and proceeding, that good works are *not* the condition for sanctification. What is necessary for sanctification is saving faith, and the kind of faith that leads to utter consecration of our whole self, as "a continual sacrifice" to God and God's will for us.

It is also important to point out that the Wesleys' view of holiness was Christocentric (Christ-centered). It is faith in Christ alone that opens the door to justification, New Birth, and sanctification. And it is the mind of Christ which is being formed within the Christian by faith, through the work of the Holy Spirit. Hence, John often preached holiness from 1 Corinthians 1:30: "Christ our wisdom and righteousness, and sanctification, and redemption."[1]

Three of John's early written sermons from the decade prior to his Aldersgate experience offer powerful descriptions of scriptural holiness or sanctification. Richard Heitzenrater has pointed out that John wrote two of these, "The Singleness of Eye," and "The One Thing Needful," during the Atlantic crossing to do missionary work in Georgia, and that Charles copied them and preached them both in America and in England. The fact that both Wesleys used these two sermons points to their relative unanimity on the doctrine of holiness.

"The Singleness of Eye" was based on Matthew 6:22-23: "The Light of the body is the eye; if therefore thine eye be single, thy whole body shall be full of light. But if thine eye be evil, thy whole body shall be full of

---

1. This sermon text appears nearly eighteen times in John's journal during the early years of the Wesleyan revival. Unfortunately, this seems to have been an extemporaneous sermon, which John preached without manuscript, and no written text survives for this message.

darkness." Charles called this sermon "A Single Intention," and the sermon register that is written into the fly leaf of the manuscript of this sermon indicates that he preached it on St. Simons Island, and in Savannah, Georgia, in 1736, and at the Castle in Oxford in 1737. Charles's journal also reports that he preached this sermon after his conversion on Pentecost 1738. The "single eye" of Matthew 6 became in the Wesleys' proclamation a metaphor for a single or unified intention to love and serve God, unreservedly from the heart. Holiness or "light" comes into the human soul through the eye-gate of utter consecration:

> The sum is this: as long as thou hast but one end in all thy thoughts, and words, and actions, to please God, or, which is all one, to improve in holiness, in the love of God, and thy neighbor; so long thou shalt clearly see what conduces thee thereto. The God whom thou servest shall so watch over thee that light, and love, and peace, shall guide all thy ways, and shine upon all thy paths. But no sooner shalt thou divide thy heart, and aim at anything besides holiness, than the light from which thou turnest away, being withdrawn, thou shalt not know whither thou goest. Ignorance, sin, and misery shall overspread thee, till thou fall headlong into utter darkness.

Based on Luke 10:42, "The One Thing Needful" provides a carefully nuanced understanding of sanctification. The "one thing needful" for all Christians is to desire that our innermost nature be changed from that which is fallen and which separates us from God to that which bears God's image and likeness. As John wrote and Charles preached, "To recover our first estate, from which we are thus fallen, is the one thing now needful — to re-exchange the image of Satan for the image of God, bondage for freedom, sickness for health. Our one business is to raise out of our souls the likeness of our destroyer, and to be born again, to be formed after the likeness of our Creator." Charles's poetical commentary on Luke 10:42 captures well the thrust of this sermon:

> Needful for the good of man
> One only thing there is,
> Here to live for God, and gain
> The everlasting bliss:
> Earth we soon shall leave behind
> Our life is as a shadow gone;

An eternal soul should mind
Eternity alone.

What is everything beside
For which the world contend?
Baits of lust, or boasts of pride,
Which in a moment end:
After earthly happiness
I can no longer pant or rove,
Need no more, who all possess
In Jesu's heart-felt love.

Even after their conversions, in some ways the Wesleys' views on holiness did not change. John's sermon "Circumcision of the Heart," based on Romans 2:29, was first preached at St. Mary's Church, in Oxford, on January 1, 1733. It was probably written just before that date. It reflects the Wesleys' sense of urgency about striving after "the holiness without which no one shall see God." This was a sermon that John reworked (perhaps) and published in 1748 in the first installment of his standard *Sermons on Several Occasions,* which indicated that John was willing to stand by what he had written and preached in his earlier, pre-conversion years. In fact, he wrote in his journal entry for September 1, 1778, "I know not that I can write a better [sermon] on *The Circumcision of the Heart* than I did five and forty years ago. Perhaps, indeed, I may have read five or six hundred books more than I had then and may know a little more history or natural philosophy than I did. But I am not sensible that this has made any essential addition to my knowledge of divinity. Forty years ago I knew and preached every Christian doctrine which I preach now."

In this sermon John stressed that "a right state of soul — a mind and spirit renewed after the image of him that created it — is one of those important truths that can only be 'spiritually discerned.'" The general term John used to describe it was "holiness," which he fleshed out in this manner: "In general we may observe it is that habitual disposition of soul which in the Sacred Writings is termed 'holiness,' and which directly implies the being cleansed from sin, 'from all filthiness both of flesh and spirit,' and by consequence the being endued with those virtues which were also in Christ Jesus, the being so 'renewed in the image of our mind' as to be 'perfect, as our Father in heaven is perfect.'"

While this process of inner renewal requires our "Singleness of Eye," the undividedness of our intentions, it is not something we can do by our-selves. The Spirit of God, by God's grace, working through our faith, works in us this marvelous work: "At the same time we are convinced that we are not sufficient of ourselves to help ourselves; that without the Spirit of God we can do nothing but add sin to sin; that it is he alone 'who worketh in us' by his almighty power; either 'to will or do' that which is good — it being as impossible for us even to think a good thought without the supernatural assistance of his Spirit as to create ourselves, or to renew our whole souls in righteousness and true holiness." Thus, at the end of his first point, John urged: "Have no end, no ultimate end, but God. Thus our Lord [said]: 'One thing is needful.' And if thine eye be singly fixed on this one thing, 'thy whole body shall be full of light.'" And John concluded the entire sermon with an urgent plea for the same focus and commitment: "Here is the sum of the perfect law: this is the true 'circumcision of the heart.' Let the spirit return to God that gave it, with the whole train of its affections. . . . Let it be continually offered up to God through Christ, in flames of holy love. And let no creatures be suffered to share with him; for he is a jealous God. His throne he will not divide with another: he will reign without a rival. . . . Desire not to live but to praise his name; let all your thoughts, words, and works tend to his glory. 'Set your heart firm on him, and on other things only as they are in and from him.' 'Let your soul be filled with so entire a love of him that you may love nothing but for his sake.'" In short, we should desire with our whole hearts to "have this mind in us which was also in Christ Jesus." This same emphasis was quite common in Charles's hymns:

> Christ the head, the corner-stone,
>   Shall be brought forth in me;
> Glory be to Christ alone,
>   His grace shall set me free!
> I shall shout my Saviour's name
>   Him I evermore shall praise,
> All the work of grace proclaim,
>   Of sanctifying grace.

Works of Piety and Works of Mercy

Having strenuously argued that we are not saved by good works, that jus-tification and sanctification are dependent upon faith alone in Christ, and with God's grace as their foundation, the Wesleys turned to the question of the role of good works. Because the process of sanctification involves the cooperation of our will with God's will, it involves both repentance in believers and good works. Our growth in grace depends upon our willingness to respond to God's grace, and to turn from our wrong actions and attitudes as God's Spirit convicts us of these shortcomings. As Albert Outler pointed out, "Indeed, since repentance means self-knowledge, the farther Christians are along the way to sanctification, the more sensitive they are to their shortfalls in faith, hope, and love." John smarted at the criticism that he taught justification by faith and sanctification by works: "it has been roundly and vehemently affirmed for these five and twenty years. But I have constantly declared just the contrary, and that in all manner of ways. I have continually testified in private and in public that we are sanctified, as well as justified, by faith. . . . Exactly as we are justified by faith, so are we sanctified by faith. Faith is the condition, and the only condition of sanctification, exactly as it is of justification." But the person who willfully neglects either repentance or good works will not grow in God's grace, will not experience Christian maturity, and will not be renewed in the image of God: "It is incumbent on all that are justified to be zealous of good works. And these are so necessary that if a man willingly neglect them, he cannot reasonably expect that he shall ever be sanctified. He cannot 'grow in grace,' in the image of God, the mind which was in Christ Jesus'; nay, he cannot retain the grace he has received, he cannot continue in faith, or in the favour of God." John concluded from this that "both repentance, rightly understood, and the practice of all good works, works of piety, as well as works of mercy (now properly so called since they spring from faith), are in some sense necessary to sanctification." Charles took a very similar position in his sermon on justification by faith, and good works, based on Titus 3:8: "This is a faithful saying, and these things I will that they affirm constantly, that they which have believed in God might be careful to maintain good works." In that sermon, Charles quoted extensively from the standard homilies of the Church of England, in order to demonstrate that the Wesleys' view of faith and good works was consistent with that of their mother church. Charles made the same point in his sermon on justification, No. 6, based on Romans 3:23-24, in which he quoted Anglican Article XII: "Albeit that good works, which are the fruits of faith, and follow after justification, cannot put away our sins, and endure the severity of God's judgment, yet are they pleasing and acceptable to God in Christ, and do spring out necessarily of a true and lively faith, insomuch that by them a lively faith may be as evidently known as a tree discerned by the fruit."

The Wesleys had a *relational* understanding of salvation. Justification by faith brought a person into relationship with God, through "pardon" and "forgiveness" that come through faith in Jesus Christ. Sanctification was the process whereby that relationship was deepened and made more vital, as the Christian became more and more Christlike, through the work of the Holy Spirit within. But a person had to cooperate with God in this process of inward renewal: "Work out your own salvation with fear and trembling. For it is God which worketh in you both to will and to do his good pleasure" (Phil. 2:12b-13).

Exploring this cooperation between God and humans in the process of sanctification, in his sermon "On Working Out Our Own Salvation," John Wesley urged: "God worketh in you; therefore you *can* work — otherwise it would be impossible. If he did not work it would be impossible for you to work out your own salvation. . . . Seeing all men are by nature not only sick, but 'dead in trespasses and sin,' it is not possible for them to do anything well till God raises them from the dead. It was impossible for Lazarus to 'come forth' till the Lord had given him life. And it is equally impossible for us to 'come' out of our sins, yea, or to make the least motion toward it, till he who hath all power in heaven and earth calls our dead souls into life." Because "God worketh in you; therefore you *must* work; you must be 'workers together with him' (they are the very words of the Apostle); otherwise he will cease working. The general rule on which his gracious dispensations invariably proceed is this: 'Unto him that hath shall be given, but from him that hath not,' that does not improve the grace already given, 'shall be taken away what he assuredly hath.'" In this regard, John Wesley quoted St. Augustine approvingly: "he that made us without ourselves, will not save us without ourselves." Wesley went on to explain: "He will not save us unless we 'save ourselves from this untoward generation'; unless we ourselves 'fight the good fight of faith, and lay hold on eternal life'; unless we 'agonize to enter in at the strait gate,' 'deny ourselves, and take up our cross daily,' and labour by every possible means, to 'make our own calling and election sure'."

In their "Large Minutes" the Wesleys detailed five spiritual disciplines incumbent upon the Methodists, and which were practiced in their societies: prayer, searching the Scriptures, the Lord's Supper, Fasting, and Christian Conference. These spiritual disciplines were described as "Means of Grace," since they helped a Christian grow in God's grace. In "The

Scripture Way of Salvation" John Wesley enumerated the same spiritual disciplines and described them as "works of piety" which are necessary for sanctification: "But what good works are those, the practice of which you affirm to be necessary to sanctification? First, all works of piety, such as public prayer, family prayer, and praying in our closet; receiving the Supper of the Lord; searching the Scriptures by hearing, reading, meditating; and using such a measure of fasting or abstinence as our bodily health allows."

The second type of good works that the Wesleys deemed necessary for sanctification were called "works of mercy": "such as feeding the hungry, clothing the naked, entertaining the stranger, visiting those that are in prison, or sick, or variously afflicted; such as the endeavouring to instruct the ignorant, to awaken the stupid sinner, to quicken the lukewarm, to confirm the wavering, to comfort the feebleminded, to succour the tempted, or contribute in any manner to the saving of souls from death." Wesley described these acts as "fruits meet for repentance, which are necessary to full sanctification."

Returning to the question about how this cooperation with God in repentance and good works connects with the concept of salvation by faith, John Wesley explained, "let a man have ever so much of this repentance, or ever so many good works, yet all this does not at all avail: he is not sanctified till he believes. But the moment he believes, with or without those fruits, yea, with more or less of this repentance, he is sanctified. Not in the *same sense;* for this repentance and these fruits are only *remotely* necessary, necessary in order to the continuance of his faith, as well as the increase of it; whereas faith is *immediately* and *directly* necessary to sanctification. It remains that faith is the only condition which is *immediately* and *proximately* necessary to sanctification." Charles Wesley's hymns evidenced this same interconnection of good works, subsequent to justification ("pardon") and sanctification ("holiness"):

> Whate'er our pardoning Lord
>   Commands, we gladly do,
> And guided by his sacred Word
>   We all his steps pursue.
> His glory our design,
>   We live our God to please;
> And rise, with filial fear divine,
>   To perfect holiness.

Holiness and Happiness

One of the distinctive emphases of Wesleyan soteriology is the interconnection of holiness (sanctification) and human happiness. This was a prominent pairing in John's published sermons and Charles's hymns:

> Saviour, on me the want bestow
> Which all that feel shall surely know
>   Their sins on earth forgiven;
> Give me to prove the kingdom mine,
> And taste, in holiness divine
>   The happiness of heaven.

The concept stems from Psalm 32:1: "Blessed is the man whose transgression is forgiven, whose sin is covered." John Wesley persistently rendered this text, perhaps following the *Book of Common Prayer* version, "Happy is the man. . . ."[2] Humans were created upright, John reminds his reader, in "The Mystery of Iniquity," "perfectly holy and perfectly happy." Thus "holiness and happiness are inseparably united." "But," he continued, "by rebelling against God he destroyed himself, lost the favour and the image of God, and entailed sin, with its attendant pain, on himself and all his posterity." Because of humanity's original identity as holy and happy — in the image of God — the loss of this image and the loss of relationship with God caused humanity great pain. Hence, the restoration of holiness brings with it increasing happiness. John explained, "It is in consequence of our knowing God loves us that we love him, and love our neighbour as ourselves. Gratitude toward our Creator cannot but produce benevolence to our fellow-creatures. The love of Christ constrains us, not only to be harmless, to do no ill to our neighbour, but to be useful, to be 'zealous of good works.'"

The love of God and neighbor, for John, summarized the essentials of true religion: "This is religion, and this is happiness, the happiness for which we were made. This begins when we begin to know God, by the teaching of his own Spirit. As soon as the Father of spirits reveals his Son in our hearts, and the Son reveals his Father, the love of God is shed abroad in our hearts; then, and not till then, are we happy." We are happy, he avers,

---

2. A passage in John Wesley's Sermon No. 7, "The Way to the Kingdom," suggests that John may have corrected this reading in the *Book of Common Prayer* and, following the Hebrew text, translated "blessed" as "happy."

because we have "constant communion with God" the Father, Son, and Holy Spirit. We are happy because the Holy Spirit works in us "heavenly tempers" — the fruit of the Spirit (Gal. 5:22). We are happy because we have an inner testimony from God the Holy Spirit that our lives and our works are pleasing unto God. And lastly, we are happy because we have liberty, and freedom from sin and sorrow, and hence from unhappiness and pain. Since happiness is a byproduct of sanctification, as Christians become more Christ-like they become happier: "their happiness still increases as they 'grow up into the measure of the stature of the fullness of Christ.'" Or has Charles put it poetically:

Write upon me the name divine,
And let thy Father's nature shine,
His image visibly expressed,
His glory pouring from my breast
O'er all my bright humanity,
Transformed into the God I see!

Inscribing with the city's name,
The heavenly, New Jerusalem,
To me the victor's title give,
Among thy glorious saints to live,
And all their happiness to know,
A citizen of heaven below.

The Love of God Shed Abroad in Our Hearts

Drawing upon the text of Romans 5:5, the Wesleys used this phrase, "the love of God shed abroad in his heart by the Holy Spirit that is given him," to describe sanctification as an infusion of God's love into the Christian's heart, soul, and life. This was one of the watershed differences between "almost a Christian" and a genuine Christian. "Almost a Christian" could not answer Wesley's rhetorical questions in an affirmative manner: "Is the love of God shed abroad in your heart? Can you cry out, 'my God and my all'? Do you desire nothing but Him? Are you happy in God?" Hence, in "Salvation by Faith," one of the basic explanations of the nature of Christian salvation is that Christians "are sealed with the Holy Spirit of promise, which is the earnest of their inheritance." Thus they have "peace with God through our Lord Jesus Christ. . . . They rejoice in hope of the glory of God. . . . And the love of God is shed abroad in their hearts through the Holy Ghost which is given unto them." God's love is a transforming, new-making love; as God's love is poured into the Christian's life, that believer becomes a new creature. "For his heart is necessarily, essentially evil, till the love of God is shed abroad therein."

Charles Wesley's famous hymn, "Love Divine, All Loves Excelling," linked this infusion of divine love with the formation of Jesus Christ within the Christian by faith. As Christ came into the Christian's life, as an infusion of divine love, so also came holiness or sanctification, until the image of God was restored in the person, and that person grew in grace until readied for heavenly glory:

> Love divine, all loves excelling,
>   Joy of heaven, to earth come down,
> Fix in us thy humble dwelling,
>   All thy faithful mercies crown!
> Jesu, thou art all compassion,
>   Pure, unbounded love thou art;
> Visit us with thy salvation!
>   Enter every trembling heart.
>
> Come, almighty to deliver,
>   Let us all thy grace receive;
> Suddenly return, and never,
>   Never more thy temples leave.
> Thee we would be always blessing,
>   Serve thee as thy hosts above,
> Pray, and praise thee without ceasing,
>   Glory in thy perfect love.
>
> Finish then thy new creation,
>   Pure and spotless let us be;
> Let us see thy great salvation
>   Perfectly restored in thee;
> Changed from glory into glory,
>   Till in heaven we take our place,
> Till we cast our crowns before thee,
>   Lost in wonder, love, and praise.

QUESTIONS FOR REFLECTION

1. Can you distinguish between justification, the New Birth, and sanctification? How would you describe each of these aspects of salvation?
2. What are "works of piety" and "works of mercy"? How do they relate to a Christian's sanctification? In what sense are they necessary for salvation?
3. Why did the Wesleys think that holiness and happiness were deeply interconnected? Do you agree?
4. Do you find the love of God "shed abroad" in your heart? Does God's love shape and transform your life?

SUGGESTIONS FOR FURTHER READING

Lindstrom, Harold. *Wesley and Sanctification* (Grand Rapids: Francis Asbury Press/Zondervan, 1980).
Wesley, Charles. Sermon No. 5, "Faith and Good Works."
Wesley, John. Sermon No. 43, "The Scripture Way of Salvation."

CHAPTER FIVE

His Pity No Exception Makes

GRACE

No man is without some preventing grace.

John Wesley, Letter, DXXIV

The Wesleys had already been Anglicans and Arminians for three generations when the Methodist Revival began in 1738-39. Charles, who spent his formative years living with his elder brother Samuel, seems to have imbibed his High Church Anglicanism and Arminian perspective from Samuel. John Wesley seems to have come by his Arminianism through the Anglican tradition, and his own forays into Holy Scripture. His father, Samuel Wesley Sr., recommended Hugo Grotius's commentary on the Old Testament to son John as he prepared for Holy Orders; Grotius was one of the founders of the Dutch Arminian tradition. But it is also clear that John's journal, which is generally quite assiduous in reporting his various reading projects, reveals little — if any — acquaintance with the writings of the Dutch Arminians. In fact, as Albert Outler points out, "Arminius himself had never been one of Wesley's decisive sources."

It seems that the Wesleys accepted the title "Arminian" almost by default. Just as they had taken a title of derision, "Methodist," and turned it into a badge of honor during their Oxford days, so also John Wesley responded to Calvinistic criticism of their theory of salvation by first publishing "What is an Arminian?" and then establishing his *Arminian Magazine* (in 1778).

"What is an Arminian?" explained his position with a calmness that certainly belied nearly forty years of disputes with Calvinist colleagues over the theology of predestination. Wesley hung the distinction between

Calvinists and Arminians on the "undeniable difference" between absolute and conditional predestination: "The Arminians hold, God has decreed, from all eternity, touching all that have the written word, 'He that believeth shall be saved; He that believeth not, shall be condemned.'" For John conditional election was the foundation for the corollary doctrines of unlimited atonement, resistible grace, and conditional perseverance. These were standard Wesleyan doctrines, but they had been hammered out on the anvil of controversy and in the face of persecution so severe that John could wryly admit: "To say, 'this man is an Arminian,' has the same effect on many hearers, as to say, 'This a mad dog.' . . . They run away from him with all diligence; and will hardly stop, unless it be to throw a stone at the dreadful and mischievous animal."

Charles Wesley encountered similar sentiments as he preached his message of unlimited atonement (Christ died for all people, not just the elect), and the universality of God's grace (all can be saved by grace if they turn to God through faith and repentance). On August 22, 1739, for example, in the midst of his preaching tour of central England, Charles wrote: "Mrs. Seward is irreconcilably angry with me; 'for he offers Christ to all.' Her maids are of the same spirit; and their Baptist teacher insists that I ought to have my [pulpit] gown stripped over my ears."

Controversy between Calvinistic and Arminian doctrines of salvation was with the Methodist movement almost from its inception. Five months after his conversion to vital Christian faith, Charles Wesley found himself enmeshed in a dispute over predestination of particular individuals to salvation, as well as the corresponding corollary beliefs that Christ died only for the elect, and that a person once saved could not lose salvation. The dispute emerged at the home of his friend John Bray. Charles's journal entry for September 22, 1738, reported: "At Bray's I expounded Eph. 1. A dispute arising about absolute predestination, I entered my protest against that doctrine." Charles preached and taught from Ephesians 1:5, that the saved are predestined to be adopted and saved through faith in Jesus Christ. That is, the *means* or condition whereby persons will be saved is what God predestined "before the foundation of the earth," not the particular identity of which persons will be saved and which persons will not. Hence, Charles and John preached a gospel of "conditional" as opposed to "absolute" predestination. They believed that God had predestined the conditions whereby women and men would be saved by faith in God's Son.

By June 29, 1739, Charles intimated that "the sower of tares is beginning to trouble us with disputes about Predestination." John Cennick, master of the Kingswood school (which the Wesleys had established in Bristol for the children of miners), was a closet Calvinist who emerged as the leader of an opposition party within Wesleyan Methodism. This opposition against the Wesleyan Arminian doctrines had solidified to the point that Charles (who was working in Bristol at this time) reported to John on December 6, 1740, that a "predestination party" had developed among the Methodists. He saw it as a potential problem, saying that "the poison of Calvin has drunk up their spirit of love." The Kingswood school became the storm center of a controversy over predestination which threatened to divide the fledgling Methodist movement. In Charles Wesley's mind, at least, it was a battleground of a great spiritual struggle.

God's Work: Prevenient or Preventing Grace

In derision, Arminians are sometimes called "Pelagians" or "Semi-Pelagians," after the ancient heresy of Pelagius (who wrote between A.D. 390-418). Pelagius did not believe in original sin, and taught that humans could be saved through an exercise of their God-given free will. As we have seen, the Wesleys *did* believe in original sin, and *did not* believe that humans are saved by free will, so it is inaccurate to associate their theology of salvation, or soteriology, with that of Pelagius.

What characterizes the Wesleys' soteriology more appropriately is their emphasis upon prevenient grace (which they sometimes called "preventing grace"). Since it is *grace,* prevenient grace is a work of God upon the human heart; it is not an act of human, unspoiled free will. Both Wesley brothers believed that God, our Seeking Father, is constantly reaching out to God's fallen children, and calling them home to faith, through the work of the Holy Spirit. As John put it, "the moment the Spirit of the Almighty strikes the heart of him that was till then without God in the world, it breaks the hardness of his heart and creates all things new. The sun of righteousness appears and shines upon his soul, showing him the light of the glory of God in the face of Jesus Christ." Thus, as John preached in another place, "Salvation begins with what is usually termed and very properly, 'preventing grace,' including the first wish to please God, the first dawn of light concerning His will, and the first slight, transient conviction of having sinned against Him."

One of the Wesleys' favorite texts for explaining the inner workings of their theory of salvation was Philippians 2:12-13: "Work out your own salvation with fear and trembling; for it is God that worketh in you, both to will and to do of his good pleasure." For them salvation was a relationship, in which God's work was embraced and followed by our work. God's work of grace, prevenient grace — which can be and too frequently is refused — must be met by our repentance and faith. Hence, in the Wesleyan view, salvation is a cooperative work, in which the Divine Will, in the Person of the Holy Spirit, comes upon our conscience or heart with the first drawing of God's grace; the Spirit works on our fallen will or in our natural conscience to the point that we can will to turn from our sin and embrace God through faith in Jesus Christ.

Because of their understanding of passages like John 16:9, "and when [the Holy Spirit] comes, he will reprove the world of sin, and of righteousness, and of judgment," the Wesleys believed that the Holy Spirit works in the hearts of all people, convicting, calling, and wooing them to come to God through faith. John stressed that the Spirit of God speaks and works in a person's conscience:

> What is conscience in the Christian sense? It is that faculty of the soul which, by the assistance of the grace of God, sees at one and the same time, (1) our own tempers [attitudes] and lives, the real nature and quality of our thoughts, words, and actions; (2) the rule whereby we are to be directed, and (3) the agreement, or disagreement therewith. To express this a little largely: conscience implies, first, the faculty a man has of knowing himself, of discerning both in general and in particular his own tempers, thoughts, words, and actions. But this is not possible for him to do without the assistance of the Spirit of God.

This is God's "work" in a person coming to faith; a prevenient work of grace, because it precedes our "work" in responding to God's grace. This inner working of the Holy Sprit, through prevenient grace, is going on in the lives of all people by virtue of their being created by God in God's image (Gen. 1:26) and by virtue of the voice of God speaking in their conscience. But God's prevenient grace can be refused. Hence, as John remarked, "no man sins because he has not grace, but because he does not use the grace which he hath."

Our Work: The Means of God's Grace

But since salvation is a relationship, we also have our "work" to do in the process of responding to God's grace. As John wrote in his sermon "On Working Out Our Own Salvation," "*Since* he [God] worketh in you of his own good pleasure, without any merit of yours, both to will and to do, *it is possible* for you to fulfill all righteousness. It is possible for you to 'love God, because he hath first loved us,' and to 'walk in love,' after the pattern of our great Master. We know indeed, that word of his to be absolutely true, 'Without me ye can do nothing.' But on the other hand we know, every believer can say, 'I can do all things through Christ that strengtheneth me.'"

So what do we need to do to cooperate with God in the working out of our own salvation? John turns to the prophet Isaiah for a "general answer touching the first steps which we are to take: 'Cease to do evil; learn to do well' [Isa. 1:16-17]." Furthermore,

> If ever you desire that God should work in you that faith whereof cometh both present and eternal salvation, by the grace already given, fly from all sin as from the face of a serpent; carefully avoid every evil word and work; yea, abstain from all appearance of evil. And "learn to do well"; be zealous of good works, of works of piety, as well as works of mercy. Use family prayer, and cry to God in secret. Fast in secret, and "your Father seeth in secret, he will reward you openly." "Search the Scriptures"; hear them in public, read them in private, and meditate therein. At every opportunity be a partaker of the Lord's Supper. "Do this in remembrance of him," and he will meet you at his own table. Let your conversation be with the children of God, and see that it "be in grace, seasoned with salt." As you have time, do good unto all men, to their souls and to their bodies. And herein "be steadfast, unmovable, always abounding in the work of the Lord." It then only remains that ye deny yourselves and take up your cross daily. Deny yourselves every pleasure which does not prepare you for taking pleasure in God, and willingly embrace every means of drawing near to God.

Thus, the Methodists embraced "the means of grace" as a part of the process of their salvation. As John wrote, "by 'means of grace,' I understand outward signs, words, or actions towards God, and appointed for this end, to be the ordinary channels whereby he might convey to men preventing, justifying or sanctifying grace."

Critiquing Calvinism

In April 1739 John Wesley preached and published a sermon entitled "Free Grace," in which he critiqued the predestinarianism that was beginning to divide the infant Methodist movement. It was a step that he took with some hesitation; in his cipher diary, for April 26th, 1739, he wrote, "appealed to God about predestination." Albert Outler reports that John even cast lots — twice — trying to ascertain God's will about taking up the critique. Wesley must have come to an affirmative conclusion, because on April 29, he preached his sermon entitled "Free Grace." John's journal reported: "I declared the *free* grace of God to about four thousand people, from those words, 'He that spared not his own Son, but delivered him up for us all, how shall he not with him also freely give us all things?' [Rom. 8:32]." His basic premise was that "The grace or love of God, whence cometh our salvation, is free in all, and free for all."

John's critique focused most of its attention upon the predestination of individuals to condemnation, which he argued is an inevitable conclusion (either explicitly or implicitly) of saying that the saved are unconditionally elected and predestined by God. The "horrible decree," as it was sometimes called, makes preaching the gospel and all of God's promises empty of effect, since there are some people ("the reprobate") for whom these do not have the potential of leading to salvation:

> Call it therefore by whatever name you please — "election," "preterition," "predestination," or "reprobation" — it comes in the end to the same thing. The sense of all is plainly this: by virtue of an eternal, unchangeable, irresistible decree of God, one part of mankind are infallibly saved, and the rest infallibly damned; it being impossible that any of the former should be damned, or that any of the latter should be saved.

This understanding of salvation makes preaching void, in Wesley's view, because "the end of preaching [is] 'to save souls' [James 5:19]. . . . And it is useless to them that are not elected." Hence, John concluded, "This then is a plain proof that the doctrine of predestination is not a doctrine of God, because it makes void the ordinance of God; and God is not divided against himself. A second is that it directly tends to destroy that holiness which is the end of all the ordinances of God."

Wesley thought predestination, explained in the hyper-Calvinistic way, which stressed double predestination (to election and reprobation), tended to eliminate the motivation for holiness, namely, "the hope of heaven and fear of hell." In a similar way he thought that this brand of Calvinism tended to "destroy several branches of holiness. Such are meekness and love: love, I mean of our enemies, of the evil and unthankful." Thirdly, John opined, "this doctrine tends to destroy the comfort of religion, the happiness of Christianity. This is evident as to all those who believe themselves to be reprobated, or who only suspect or fear it. All the great and precious promises are lost to them. They afford them no ray of comfort." "Fourthly, this uncomfortable doctrine directly tends to destroy our zeal for good works." And "fifthly, this doctrine not only tends to destroy Christian holiness, happiness, and good works, but hath also a direct and manifest tendency to overthrow the whole Christian revelation." John meant by this that if a person is saved or damned by the eternal and irreversible decree of God, there is no particular need to hear and affirm the promises of the gospel of Jesus Christ. Hence, "In making the gospel thus unnecessary to all sorts of men you give up the whole Christian cause." And finally, Wesley argued, heatedly, that the doctrine of eternal reprobation misrepresents Jesus Christ and our loving God, both of whom have revealed that they would that no one should perish, but have eternal life. Hence, John proclaimed: "This is the blasphemy clearly contained in 'the horrible decree' of predestination. And here I fix my foot. On this I join issue with every asserter of it. You represent God as worse than the devil — more false, more cruel, more unjust. But you say you will 'prove it by Scripture.' Hold! What will you prove by Scripture? That God is worse than the devil?"

George Whitefield and Selina Hastings, the Countess of Huntingdon, both of whom were Calvinistic Methodists and friends and colleagues of the Wesley brothers, were deeply offended and angered by John's sermon. Thus began a preaching and pamphlet war between the Calvinist (Whitefieldite) and Arminian (Wesleyan) wings of the Methodist movement. In a letter written in late 1741, George Whitefield complained to John Wesley, "Dear Brother Charles is more and more rash. He has lately printed some very bad hymns." Charles had just returned from a very successful preaching tour of Wales, where he had this insight: "Who can resist the power of love? A loving messenger of a loving God might drive reprobation out of Wales, without once naming it." The "bad hymns" were Charles's *Hymns on God's Everlasting Love* — hymns which had the explicit intention of contradicting the Calvinistic understanding of predestination and its theological corollaries. These hymns were so successful, from a Wesleyan point of view, that two separate collections were released under the same title. The first hymnbook contained fourteen pieces, written in a great variety of meters and poetic feet. The title of the book was aptly explained in its first offering:

1. Father, whose *Everlasting Love*
    Thy only Son for sinners gave,
      Whose grace to *all* did *freely* move,
    And sent Him down a *world to save.*

2. Help us Thy mercy to extol,
    Immense, unfathom'd, unconfined;
      To praise the Lamb who died for *all,*
    The general Saviour of all mankind.

3. *Thy undistinguishing regard*
    Was cast on Adam's fallen race;
      For all thou hast in Christ prepared
    Sufficient, sovereign, saving grace.

4. Jesus hath said, we *all* shall hope,
      Preventing grace for all is free;
    "And I, if I be lifted up,
      I will *draw all men* unto me."

The theological thrust of both hymnals was firmly established in this first hymn; "everlasting love" quickly became a Wesleyan synonym for the gospel of unlimited atonement (Jesus died for all people) and prevenient grace. The first hymn in this collection contained seventeen verses, and made the main point of the hymns in both collections when it affirmed more than twenty-three times that Jesus Christ died for "all" people.

Charles Wesley's emphasis upon the unlimited atonement had important theological corollaries. The first was conditional election. Since Christ has died for all, God has not chosen certain individuals, from among the fallen human race, to be given salvation, thereby passing by or damning those not chosen. Salvation is conditional insofar as one must will to receive it by faith. For Charles the distinction between the saved and the lost lay not with God or Jesus Christ ("the Lamb"), but with a reluctance in the human will:

7. Behold the Lamb of God, who takes
   The sins of all the world away!
   His pity no exception makes;
   But all that *will* receive Him *may.*

A second important theological element in the Wesleys' gospel of "everlasting love" was their emphasis upon "free grace," which implied the universal offer of the gospel of God's acceptance:

3. Free as air Thy mercy streams,
   Thy universal grace
   Shines with undistinguish'd beams
   On all the fallen race;
   All from Thee a power receive
   To reject, or hear, Thy call;
   All may choose to die, or live;
   Thy grace is free for all.

"Free grace" was an enabling grace, which Charles termed "preventing grace" or "assisting grace." He described the way this grace opened the path to God by an analogy based on the text of Psalm 5:7:

ASSISTED by preventing grace,
I bow me toward the holy place,
Faintly begin my God to fear,
His weak, external worshipper;
But if my Lord His blood apply,
Entering into the holiest I
Boldly approach my Father's throne,
And claim Him all in Christ my own.

The "assistance" of prevenient grace was a necessary precondition to reconciliation with God, since "unassisted by Thy grace,/We can only evil do;/Wretched is the human race,/Wretched more than words can show,/Till Thy blessing from above,/Tells our hearts that God is love." In a similar way, grace is "pro'fer'd" in the imagery of the Waiting Father (Luke 15:11ff.), who spreads his arms wide to receive the return of the prodigal child: "Open are Thy arms to embrace/Me, the worst of rebels me;/*All in me the hindrance lies,*/Call'd I still refuse to rise." Hence, the *Hymns on*

God's Everlasting Love contrast the Wesleyan concept of prevenient grace with the Calvinistic electing grace (called "damning grace") to emphatically argue that "Grace doth more than sin abound;/Thy grace is free for all,/[that] Salvation *might* be found." The balance point between unlimited atonement and "free grace" was Wesley's doctrine of conditional election, which locates the distinction between the saved and the lost within the responsibility of the person who has been prepared for salvation by prevenient grace. The fourth verse of the same poem cited above makes this point well: "All in me the hindrance lies."

Charles's first edition of *Hymns on God's Everlasting Love* carried two very polemical hymns, at the end, which clearly surpassed the others in mounting a stinging counteroffensive against the doctrines of Calvinism. The first of these polemical pieces was "The Cry of a Reprobate." Wesley's spokesman in this hymn presented his spiritual autobiography: "By my own sin betray'd and bound,/A sheep I to the slaughter go." The intention of Charles's hymn was to persuade by counterexample, and to enforce the evangelist's calls for the decision of saving faith. The singer, having heard the account of the reprobate's self-damnation and having examined the prospect of hell, which was painted in the hymn, ought to repent and turn to God to receive the salvation God offers. Thus the "Cry of a Reprobate" evangelizes the singer by continuing Charles Wesley's emphasis upon conditional election and free grace, applying them in an even more dramatic form. The hymn concludes with the reprobate resolutely accepting responsibility:

> By my own hands, not His, I fall,
> The hellish doctrine I disprove;
> Sinner, His grace is free for all;
> Though I am damn'd yet God is love.

The "hellish doctrine" disproved in the reprobate's self-damnation is, of course, the Calvinistic doctrine of absolute predestination to reprobation. Wesley's solution to the dilemma of affirming the juridical justice of God in condemning the guilty and yet affirming that God is love was found in the sinner's willful rejection of God's loving call to salvation.

The second overtly polemical hymn in this same collection was titled "The Horrible Decree." It is a thoroughgoing attack upon the notion of predestination of persons to damnation. In this heated hymn the writer established a double dialogue, which alternated between his spokesman and Christ, or between his spokesman and adherents of the Calvinistic position on election and predestination. Charles showed familiarity with his opponents' theological language, and utilized several of their doctrinal catchphrases to attack their own point of view:

1. Ah! Gentle, gracious Dove;
   And art Thou grieved in me,
   That sinners should restrain Thy love,
   And say, "It is not free;
   It is not free for ALL;
   The MOST THOU PASSEST BY,
   And mockest with a fruitless call
   Whom Thou hast doom'd to die."

2. They think Thee NOT SINCERE
   In giving each his day;
   "THOU ONLY DRAW'ST THE SINNER NEAR,
   TO CAST HIM QUITE AWAY.
   TO AGGRAVATE HIS SIN,
   HIS SURE DAMNATION SEAL,
   THOU SHOW'ST HIM HEAVEN, AND SAY'ST GO IN —
   AND THRUSTS HIM INTO HELL."

3. O HORRIBLE DECREE,
   Worthy of whence it came!
   Forgive their hellish blasphemy
   Who charge it on the Lamb,
   Whose pity Him inclined
   To leave His throne above,
   The Friend and Saviour of mankind,
   The God of grace and love.

The second series of *Hymns on God's Everlasting Love* continued with the same emphasis as the first series: stress upon God's all-inclusive love. It also carried on the strongly polemical tone earlier established in hymns like "The Horrible Decree." Hymn No. 13 in the second series, "The Lord's Controversy," is particularly interesting, since in it the predestination controversy has become "The Lord's Controversy," in which the ministers of true religion struggle against "The Priest of Moloch" — whose heretical views were once again attacked by using (and sometimes misusing) their own theological language. It is no wonder that George Whitefield, the apostle of Calvinistic Methodism, disapproved of these hymns!

The predestination controversy had the effect of sharpening the Wesleys' Arminian understanding of salvation. It not only drew forth from them polemical sermons and heated hymns, it caused them to stress more concretely and more completely a theology of love as one of the most characteristic expressions of their version of the gospel. The Wesleys and their descendants would have certainly championed conditional election, unlimited atonement, and a grace that was "free" — both prevenient and resistible — without the early predestination controversies, but this controversy with their Calvinistic colleagues sharpened and honed the Wesleys' theology of "free grace" and "everlasting love."

QUESTIONS FOR REFLECTION

1. What is the role of "prevenient grace" in the Wesleys' theology of salvation?
2. In what sense is salvation by "grace alone"? In what sense is salvation, as the Wesleys described it, not by grace alone?
3. Can you distinguish between the Wesleys' Arminian approach to salvation by grace and that of their Calvinistic contemporaries?
4. What were the effects of the "Calvinistic controversy" upon the early Wesleyan movement and its view of salvation?

SUGGESTIONS FOR FURTHER READING

Coppedge, Alan. *Shaping Wesleyan Theology: John Wesley in Theological Debate* (Nappanee, Ind.: Evangel Press, 1987).
Davies, Horton. "Charles Wesley and the Calvinist Tradition," in S. T. Kimbrough, ed., *Charles Wesley: Poet and Theologian* (Nashville: Kingswood Books, 1992), pp. 186-205.
Wesley, Charles. *Hymns on God's Everlasting Love.*
Wesley, John. Sermon No. 110, "Free Grace."

CHAPTER SIX

The Promised Paraclete Is Given

THE HOLY SPIRIT

Assembled here with one accord
Calmly we wait the promised grace,
  The purchase of our dying Lord —
Come, Holy Ghost, and fill the place.

Hymn for the Day of Pentecost

It comes as no great surprise that the Wesley brothers affirmed the doctrine of the Holy Spirit as a theological verity that had been bequeathed to them by both Scripture and the Christian tradition. As Charles described the situation in one of his hymns, they were "fix'd on the *Athanasian* mound." By this he meant that they embraced the robust Trinitarian theology (which includes the Holy Spirit) enshrined in the work of St. Athanasius and the Nicene Creed. When John prepared "Articles of Religion" for the infant American Methodist Church in 1784, he affirmed the Anglican Article Five, and adopted it as Methodist Article Four.[1] John's New Testament "Note" on John 15:26 makes it clear that he thought of the Holy Spirit as a full-fledged divine Person who replaced the presence of the ascended Jesus Christ, and not simply as the life-force or an impersonal being:

The Spirit's coming, and being sent by our Lord from the Father, to testify of Him, are personal characteristics, and plainly distinguish Him

---

1. *United Methodist Book of Discipline*, 2008, Article IV: On the Holy Ghost: "The Holy Ghost, proceeding from the Father and the Son, is of one substance, majesty, and glory with the Father and the Son, very and eternal God."

from the Father and the Son; and His title as *Spirit of Truth,* together with His *proceeding from the Father,* can agree to none but a divine person. And that he proceeds from the Son, as well as from the Father, may be fairly argued from His being called *the Spirit of Christ* (1 Pet. 1:11), and from His being sent by *Christ from the Father,* as well as sent by the Father *in His name.*

This passage also points out a second important aspect of the Wesleyan approach to the doctrine of the Holy Spirit: the utterly Christocentric (Christ-centered) nature of their formulation of the doctrine. Receiving the Holy Spirit was synonymous with receiving Jesus Christ: "Jesus, the gift divine I know,/The gift divine I ask of thee;/That living water now bestow,/Thy Spirit and thyself on me. Thou, Lord, of life the fountain art;/Now let me find thee in my heart." The role of the Holy Spirit (alternately called the Spirit of Christ) was to make the ascended Jesus Christ present in the lives of his disciples:

> He doth in all His saints reside,
>> The promised PARACLETE is given,
> The Saviour's word is verified,
>> The Holy Ghost sent down from heaven.

> We for Thy fleshly presence here
>> The presence of Thy Spirit receive,
> That everlasting Comforter
>> Doth still in all His people live.

As we will see, the work of the Holy Spirit is consistently related to the work of Jesus Christ and the task of applying the grace of Christ to a person's life. Both brothers preferred not to write about the Holy Spirit in abstract terms; instead they described the role of the Spirit in the experience of Christian life. John was able, based upon Scripture and Christian experience, to describe *how* one could discern the Holy Spirit's operation in one's Christian life:

(1) The fruit of His ordinary influences are love, joy, peace, long-suffering, gentleness, meekness.

(2) Whosoever has these, inwardly feels them; and if he understands his Bible, he discerns from whence they come. Observe, what he inwardly

feels is these fruits themselves; whence they come to be he learns from the Bible.

Charles Wesley experienced his own evangelical conversion on Pentecost Sunday ("Whitsunday") 1738. While both brothers turned repeatedly to the role of the Holy Spirit to explain the inner workings of salvation and Christian life, Charles's hymns and sermons show a particularly strong affinity for the person and work of the Holy Spirit — no doubt because of the connection between Pentecost and his personal faith. This proclivity is easily seen in Charles's hymns — most especially those he composed with Pentecost in mind, like *Hymns for Whitsunday* (1746) — but it is also clear in his sermons. In those extant sermons Charles preached prior to 1738 there is no mention of the work and person of the Holy Spirit, but the sermons Charles wrote and preached after his "personal Pentecost" are replete with references to the Holy Spirit and explanations of the Holy Spirit's work in Christians.

The Wesleyan doctrine of the Holy Spirit, with its grounding in the classical doctrine of the Holy Trinity, is especially remarkable given that the Wesleys lived in a time when Deism was intellectually fashionable. Charles took pains to shore up Trinitarian doctrine in his hymns:

> When'er our day of Pentecost
>   Is fully come, we surely know
> The Father, Son, and Holy Ghost
>   Our God, is manifest below:
> The Son doth in the Father dwell,
>   The Father in His Son imparts
> His Spirit of joy unspeakable,
>   And lives for ever in our hearts.
>
> Our hearts then convinced indeed
>   That Christ is with the Father One;
> The Spirit that doth from Both proceed,
>   Attests the co-eternal Son;
> The Spirit of truth and holiness
>   Asserts His own Divinity:
> And then the orthodox confess
>   One generous God in persons three.

The Holy Spirit and Prevenient Grace

The Wesleys believed that all people have within their conscience a witness to the presence and call of God upon their life. The conscience becomes a kind of loudspeaker through which the God the Holy Spirit addresses people in their inner self:

> . . . there is no man, unless he has quenched the Spirit, that is wholly void of the grace of God. No man living is entirely destitute of what is vulgarly called *natural conscience.* But this is not natural: it is more properly termed *preventing grace.* Every man has a greater or lesser measure of this, which waiteth not for the call of man. Every man has, sooner or later, good desires, although the generality of men stifle them before they can strike deep root, or produce any considerable fruit. Everyone has some measure of that light, some faint glimmering ray, which sooner or later, more or less, enlightens everyman that cometh into the world. And everyone, unless he be of the small number whose conscience is seared as with hot iron, feels more or less uneasy when he acts contrary to the light of his own conscience. So that no man sins because he has not grace, but because he does not use the grace which he hath.

Based on the affirmations of Scriptures like John 16:7-8, the Wesleys attributed this "convicting" or "convincing" role to the work of the Holy Spirit. The Scripture text gives the Holy Spirit a threefold office: to convict (or "reprove") the world of sin, righteousness, and judgment. Hence in his hymn no. 17, "For Whitsunday," Charles wrote:

1. ETERNAL PARACLETE, descend,
    Thou gift and promise of our Lord,
   To every soul, till time shall end,
    Thy succour, and Thyself afford,
   Convince, convert us, and inspire;
   Come, and baptize the world with fire.

2. Come and display the power below,
    And work Thy threefold work of grace:
   Compel mankind themselves to know,
    Convince of sin the'apostate race,

Brood o'er the deep of nature's night,
And speak again, Let there be light.

Or as Charles proclaimed in his sermon on Romans 3:23-25, "The Scripture hath concluded all under sin. To convince the world of this, is the first office of the Holy Spirit; and when a man is truly convinced of sin, then and not till then, may he be convinced of righteousness also, even the righteousness of God which is by faith in Jesus Christ unto all and upon all them that believe." Since, as we noted in a previous chapter, repentance is essentially self-knowledge with respect to one's sin, the Holy Spirit brings the awareness of sin to the human conscience in a manner that allows one to repent and thereby be justified by faith in Jesus Christ. Thus the convicted sinner says — in the words of the apostle — " 'I see another law in my members, warring against the law of my mind, and bringing me into captivity to the law of sin, which is in my members. Oh! Wretched man that I am, who shall deliver me from the body of this death?' [Rom. 7:24] Such is the language of one whom the Holy Spirit has reproved of sin, but not rescued from it."

Another example of the Holy Spirit's convicting work is seen in John Wesley's sermon "The Spirit of Bondage and of Adoption." Here John wrote: "By some awful providence, or by his Word applied with the demonstration of his Spirit, God touches the heart of him that lay asleep in darkness and in the shadow of death. He is terribly shaken out of his sleep, and awakes to a consciousness of his danger. Perhaps in a moment, perhaps by degrees, the eyes of his understanding are opened."

Reconciliation with God takes place, as Charles describes it in his conversion hymns, when the Holy Spirit sprinkles "the atoning blood" of Jesus Christ upon the heart of the repentant sinner:

Come, Holy Ghost, all quickening fire,
Come and my consecrated heart inspire,
    Sprinkled with the atoning blood:
Still to my soul Thyself reveal;
Thy mighty working may I feel,
    And know that I am one with God.

Preaching from Romans 8:1, "There is therefore now no condemnation to them which are in Christ Jesus, who walk not after the flesh, but after the Spirit," John reported: "By 'them which are in Christ Jesus' St. Paul evidently means those who truly believe in him; those who 'being justified by faith have peace with God, through our Lord Jesus Christ.' They who thus believe no longer 'walketh after the flesh,' no longer follow the motions of corrupt nature, but 'after the Spirit.' Both their thoughts, words, and works are under the direction of the Spirit of God." Hence, John urged, "'There is now no condemnation' to these. There is no condemnation to them from God, for he hath 'justified them freely by his grace,' through the redemption that is in Jesus. And there is no condemnation to them within, for they 'have received, not the spirit of the world, but the Spirit which is of God,' that they might know the things which are freely given to them of God." In a similar way, Charles believed that it is the work of the Holy Spirit that allows people to see that their sins are forgiven in Jesus Christ, and confess the Lordship of Christ in their lives:

1. Spirit of faith, come down,
   Reveal the things of God,
 And make to us the Godhead known,
   And witness with the blood:
   'Tis thine the blood to apply,
   And give us eyes to see,
 Who did for every sinner die
   Hath surely died for me.

2. No man can truly say
   That Jesus is the Lord
 Unless thou take the veil away,
   And breathe the living word;
   Then, only then we feel
   Our interest in his blood,
 And cry with joy unspeakable,
   Thou art my Lord, my God!

The Holy Spirit and New Birth

The way for justification by faith is prepared by the Holy Spirit, who woos and calls us (through prevenient grace) to return to God our Father, like the prodigal children we are. The change of our standing with God (justification) results in a "relative" change in us. As John Wesley explained, "at the same time that we are justified, yea, in that very moment, *sanctifi-*

cation begins. In that instant we are 'born again,' 'born from above,' 'born of the Spirit.' There is a *real* as well as a *relative* change. We are inwardly renewed by the power of God. We feel the 'love of God shed abroad in our heart by the Holy Ghost which is given to us.'" This process of change is begun with the New Birth, and is completed over the long haul in the work of sanctification; both the New Birth and sanctification are works of the Holy Spirit.

Indeed, Charles Wesley's famous Oxford sermon, "Awake, Thou That Sleepest" (1742), described "pure religion" and "being a Christian" as nothing other than the reception of the Holy Spirit:

> . . . on the authority of God's Word and our own Church I must repeat the question, "Hast thou received the Holy Ghost?" If thou hast not thou art not yet a Christian; for a Christian is a man that is "anointed with the Holy Ghost and with power." Thou art not yet made a partaker of pure religion and undefiled. Dost thou know what religion is? That it is a "participation in the divine nature," the life of God in the soul of man: "Christ in thee, the hope of glory"; "Christ formed in thy heart," happiness and holiness; heaven begun upon earth; a "kingdom of God within thee," "not meat and drink," no outward thing, "but righteousness and peace, and joy in the Holy Ghost"; an everlasting kingdom brought into thy soul, a "peace of God that passeth all understanding"; a "joy unspeakable and full of glory"?

Charles's basic point is quite clear: the New Birth is synonymous with the reception of the Holy Spirit, and when a person receives the Holy Spirit the life of God is begun to be formed within that person. Hence, as Charles explained later on in the same sermon, "Ye see your calling, brethren, we are called to be 'an habitation of God through his Holy Spirit,' and through his Spirit dwelling in us 'to be saints' here and partakers of the inheritance of the 'saints in light.'"

The Witness of the Spirit

John Wesley wrote and published two sermons, each entitled "The Witness of the Spirit," based on Romans 8:16, "The Spirit itself beareth witness with our spirit that we are the children of God." While separated by twenty years and written to answer differing concerns, these two sermons form a unified statement of the Wesleyan doctrine of assurance. While the first homily was deeply concerned to show that the Methodists are not "enthusiasts" — which in eighteenth-century English parlance meant something like "witless religious fanatics" — both treatises are primarily about the doctrine of assurance. They seek, implicitly, to answer the question: "How do I know that I am saved?"

The question of assurance loomed large in the spiritual pilgrimage of both Wesley brothers. In fact, it is possible to view their conversion experiences as primarily about receiving an inward assurance of their acceptance by God. Both brothers knew and intellectually embraced justification by faith alone; they simply lacked (as the Moravians put it) a "faith they could feel." Charles's personal Pentecost and John's Aldersgate Street experience brought that kind of assurance into their spiritual lives. It is no surprise that assurance became a bright star in the Wesleyan constellation of theological ideas.

John's first treatise, from 1746, defined the "Witness of the Spirit" in these terms: "the testimony of the Spirit is an inward impression on the soul, whereby the Spirit of God directly 'witnesses to my spirit that I am a child of God'; that Jesus Christ hath loved me, and given himself for me; that all my sins are blotted out, and I, even I, am reconciled to God." This *direct* witness is described as an "inward impression"; it is a feeling given by the Holy Spirit that a person is loved and has been accepted by God. This testimony or witness of the Spirit precedes "the testimony of our own spirit." God works within the human soul, and that work is felt or experienced by the person in whom the spiritual work is undertaken. John described the relationship between the witness of the Spirit and the witness of our own spirit:

> That this "testimony of the Spirit of God" must needs, in the very nature of things, be antecedent to the "testimony of our own spirit" may appear from this single consideration: we must be holy of heart and holy in life before we can be conscious that we are so, inwardly and outwardly holy. . . . Since therefore this "testimony of his Spirit" must precede the love of God and all holiness, of consequence it must precede our inward consciousness thereof, or the "testimony of our spirit" concerning them.

This then leads to the *indirect* witness of the Spirit. After the Holy Spirit works in our inward life, we have an inward impression that we are born of God. From that inner work stem godly virtues like holiness and love of God. We are able to discern that we have in our spirit a hunger for holiness and a love for God; this is a direct result of the Holy Spirit's presence in our lives, and indirect evidence that we belong to God. In a later portion of that same sermon, John Wesley put it this way: "He that now loves God — that delights and rejoices in him with an humble joy, an holy delight, and an obedient love — is a child of God; But I thus love, delight, and rejoice in God; therefore I am a child of God; then a Christian can in no wise doubt of his being a child of God."

Charles Wesley's *Hymns for Whitsunday* (1746) also speak powerfully of the assurance Christians have through the inner work of the Holy Spirit. In this hymn assurance is described as the "second function" of the Comforter:

> 4. His blessing love 'tis Thine to seal
>   With pardon on the contrite heart:
>   To us, to us the grace reveal,
>   The righteousness impute, impart;
>   Discharge Thy second function here,
>   And now descend the Comforter.

> 5. The righteousness of Christ our Lord
>   For pardon of our sins, declare,
>   Inspeak the everlasting word
>   That freely justified we are,
>   By grace received and brought to God,
>   And saved through faith in Jesu's blood.

Charles Wesley's sermon "Awake, Thou That Sleepest" described the presence of the Holy Spirit in a person's life as "an experimental [or experiential] knowledge" of Christ: "This is eternal life, to know the only true God and Jesus Christ Whom he hath sent. This experimental knowledge, and this alone, is true Christianity. He is a Christian who hath received the Spirit of Christ. He is not a Christian who hath not received him. Neither is it possible to have received him and not know it."

The Holy Spirit and Sanctification

As we saw in a previous chapter, *sanctification* describes the process of becoming holy. This process begins immediately after we have been justified by faith in Jesus Christ. Wesley described justification as what God does "for us" in Jesus Christ, and sanctification (or the New Birth) as what God does "in us" through faith in Jesus Christ. In his sermon "The Scripture Way of Salvation," John wrote, "At the same time we are justified, yea, in that very moment, *sanctification* begins. In that instant we are 'born again,' 'born from above,' 'born of the Spirit.'" One receives the Holy Spirit when one is justified, and that reception marks the beginning of New Birth and sanctification.

The work of the Holy Spirit is not a one-time event, however. The Spirit continues to refine, renew, convict, and convert the inner and outer life of Christians as long as they abide in faith. Christians are spiritual construction (or reconstruction) projects, being remade and renewed in the image of Christ. For this reason, many of Charles's hymns depict Christians as "Groaning for full Redemption" — longing and praying for the time when they will be made completely pure and free from the power of sin in their lives. Charles prayed,

8. O that it now from heaven might fall,
   And all my sins consume!
   Come, Holy Ghost, for thee I call,
   Spirit of burning, come!

9. Refining fire, go through my heart,
   Illuminate my soul,
   Scatter thy life through every part,
   And sanctify the whole.

10. Sorrow and sin shall then expire,
    While, entered into rest,
    I only live my God t'admire —
    My God forever blest.

Charles's *Hymns for Whitsunday* were replete with this same message. The process of sanctification begins as the "Fruits of the Spirit" (Hymn #25) are being grown in Christians by the Holy Spirit: "Root up every bitter root./ Multiply the Spirit's fruit./Love, and joy, and quiet peace,/Meek, long-suffering gentleness;/. . . All the mind which was in Thee." The following hymn looks ahead to the great future day of re-creation:

1. Then the whole earth again shall rest,
    And see its paradise restored;
   Then every soul in Jesus bless'd
    Shall bear the image of its Lord,
   In finish'd holiness renew'd,
   Immeasurably fill'd with God.

2. Spirit of sanctifying grace,
    Hasten that happy gospel day;
   Come and restore the fallen race,
    Purge all our filth and blood away,
   Our inmost soul redeem, repair,
   And fix Thy seat of judgment there.

3. Judgment to execute is Thine,
    To kill and save is Thine alone;
   Exert that energy Divine,
    Set up the everlasting throne,
   The inward kingdom from above,
   The glorious power of perfect love.

4. O wouldst Thou bring the final scene,
    Accomplish the redeeming plan,
   Thy great millennial reign begin;
    That every ransom'd child of man,
   That every soul may bow the knee,
   And rise, to reign with God in Thee.

The Holy Spirit, the Bible, and the Means

The Wesleys believed that Holy Spirit who gave the inspired Scriptures continues to speak to us through the Bible. As John Wesley put it, "The Spirit of God not only once inspired those who wrote it but continually inspires, supernaturally assists, those that read it with earnest prayer." Or as Charles wrote in one of his hymns, "The meaning of the written word/ Is still by inspiration given,/Thou only dost Thyself explain/The secret mind of God to man./Come then, Divine Interpreter,/The Scriptures to our hearts apply."

The Wesleys also believed that the Holy Spirit works good in the lives of believers through their use of spiritual disciplines, which they termed "the means of grace." They admitted "that all outward means whatever, if separate from the Spirit of God, cannot profit at all, cannot conduce in any degree either to the knowledge or love of God." But the Wesleys believed that at least five spiritual disciplines — prayer, Scripture reading, the Lord's Supper, fasting, and Christian conference — were ordained by the Scriptures as channels whereby the Holy Spirit could work good in the lives of believers. Still, they cautioned, "Settle this in your heart, that the *opus operatum,* the mere work done, profiteth nothing; that there is no *power* to save but in the Spirit of God, no *merit* but in the blood of Christ." *Opus operatum* describes the medieval belief that a sacrament or discipline "works" because it is performed properly. In contrast to this approach, the Wesleys stressed that the spiritual intention and justification by faith in the merits of Christ give "the means" their power. Charles's hymn "The Love Feast" (1739) made the same point in verse three of Part One:

> Plead we thus for faith *alone,*
> Faith which by our works is shown;
> God it is who justifies,
> Only faith the grace *applies* —
> Active faith that lives within,
> Conquers hell, and death, and sin,
> Hallows whom it first made whole,
> Forms the Saviour in the soul.

The Wesley brothers saw that the Holy Spirit is the presence of God and Jesus Christ indwelling the Christian's life. The Spirit not only applies the merits of Christ to us, through our faith in Jesus Christ, but is also said to "convince" and "convert us all" so that we come to faith ("enable us to trust") and experience a kind of assurance (the witness of the Spirit) as we "Forgiveness through His blood [may] feel."

> 1. Spirit of Faith, on Thee we call,
>   The merits of our Lord apply,
>   Convince, and then convert us all,
>   Condemn, and freely justify;
>   Set forth the all-atoning Lamb,
>   And spread the powers of Jesu's name.

2. Jesus the merciful and just
   To every heart of man reveal,
   In Him enable us to trust,
   Forgiveness through His blood to feel;
   Let all in Him redemption find;
   Sprinkle the blood on all mankind.

The Holy Spirit is also our sanctifier, a refining fire that purifies our heart, mind, soul, and life, who forms the image of God as the mind of Christ within us. The Spirit works in our lives through the Word of God and the means of grace, but the Holy Spirit is also our sovereign God, free to work in our consciences apart from the Word of God and the means of grace.

QUESTIONS FOR DISCUSSION

1. What is the connection between the Holy Spirit and prevenient grace?
2. What role does the Holy Spirit play in justification? In New Birth?
3. What is the Holy Spirit's role in the process of our sanctification?
4. What is "the witness of the Spirit"? Can you distinguish between the "direct" and "indirect" witness?
5. How does the Holy Spirit work in our life?

SUGGESTIONS FOR FURTHER READING

Rattenbury, John Ernest. *The Evangelical Doctrines of Charles Wesley's Hymns* (London: Epworth Press, 1941), chapter 9, "The Holy Spirit."

Starkey, Lycurgus M. *The Work of The Holy Spirit: A Study in Wesleyan Theology* (New York & Nashville: Abingdon Press, 1962).

Wesley, John. Sermon I, "The Witness of the Spirit," Pt. I, Pt. II, in *The Works of John Wesley,* ed. Albert Outler (Nashville: Abingdon Press, 1984), pp. 267-99.

CHAPTER SEVEN

Risen with Healing in His Wings

JESUS CHRIST

Join, earth and heaven, to bless
The *Lord our Righteousness*!
Mystery of redemption this,
This the Saviour's strange design,
Man's offense was counted His,
Ours is righteousness Divine.

Poetical Works, I:151

In his standard sermon No. 20, "The Lord Our Righteousness," John Wesley described the "one very considerable article of truth contained in the words recited above" as "a truth that enters deep into the nature of Christianity, and in a manner supports the whole frame of it. Of this undoubtedly may be affirmed what Luther affirms of a truth closely connected with it: it is *articulus stantis vel cadentis ecclesiae* — the Christian church stands or falls with it." Christology, the theology of the person and work of Jesus Christ, is the very foundation of Christian theology. It is the foundation upon which everything distinctive and significant about the Christian faith stands or falls.

The Wesley brothers keenly recognized and affirmed this fact, and yet because they, especially John, did not always address the issues of Christology directly, there has been considerable academic debate about how to best interpret John Wesley's Christology. Both Wesleys wrote Christology in the larger context of the theology of salvation (soteriology). They did not treat Jesus Christ's person apart from the Lord's saving work; hence John wrote no sermons which directly address the person and work of Jesus Christ. So when we try to reconstruct John's theology of Christ, we

80

look at bits of information about Jesus Christ that John gave in sermons that are primarily about salvation. For this reason, the main book-length treatment of John Wesley's Christology, by John Deschner, is based almost entirely upon an intensive study of John's *Notes Upon the New Testament.* If we ask ourselves *why* the Wesleys addressed Christology primarily in the larger context of soteriology, we have moved into an area of speculation, but this connection between Christology and soteriology does seem to fit well the task of Christian evangelists who were determined "to reform the nation, especially the church, and to spread Scriptural holiness across the land." Also, in the larger context of the academic world of English Deism, an emphasis on the true Divinity and saving efficacy of Jesus Christ might be expected from men who were determined to be — as John described them — "Bible Christians."

Jesus: God and Man

Debates about the twofold nature of Jesus Christ did not originate in the church of the Wesleys' day; they reached all the way back to the ancient church, and the controversies that led up to the council of Nicea (A.D. 325) and the formulation of the Nicene Creed. In the midst of those debates Athanasius of Alexandria (296-373) emerged as the champion of a Christology that affirmed the full humanity and the full deity of Jesus Christ over against Arianism, which described Jesus as being somewhat less than God and somewhat more than a mere man. Athanasius expressed his views in *De Incarnation Verbi Dei,* and they eventually became enshrined in the Nicene Creed. So when Charles Wesley averred that they were "fix'd on the *Athanasian* mound," he also meant that the Wesleys were rooted in the theology of the full humanity and full divinity of Jesus Christ as advocated for by Athanasius and as affirmed by the Nicene Creed.[1] John Wesley ap-

---

1. Article Two of the Nicene Creed: "We believe in one Lord, Jesus Christ, the only Son of God, eternally begotten of the Father, God from God, Light from Light, true God from true God, begotten not made, of one Being with the Father; through him all things were made. For us and for our salvation, he came down from heaven, was incarnate of the Holy Spirit and the Virgin Mary and became truly human. For our sake he was crucified under Pontius Pilate; he suffered death and was buried. On the third day, he rose again in accordance with the Scriptures; he ascended into heaven and is seated at the right hand of the Father. He will come again in glory to judge the living and the dead, and his kingdom will have no end."

proached the theological precision of the ancient creeds on this topic when he drafted "Twenty-Five Articles of Religion" for the American Methodist Church in 1784. "Article II — Of the Word, or Son of God, Who Was Made Very Man," followed the Anglican *Book of Common Prayer,* and made this affirmation:

> The Son, who is the Word of the Father, the very and eternal God, of one substance with the Father, took man's nature in the womb of the blessed Virgin; so that two whole and perfect natures, that is to say, the Godhead and Manhood, were joined together in one person, never to be divided; whereof is one Christ, very God and very Man, who truly suffered, was crucified, dead, and buried, to reconcile his Father to us, and to be a sacrifice, not only for original guilt, but also for actual sins of men.

This article of faith participates in and includes many of the great phrases of the ancient Christian creeds. Here we see Wesley's reverence for Scripture and tradition at work in his Christology. This affirmation established the American church solidly upon the foundations provided by a classical Christology. It was the sort of full and robust Christology which both brothers advocated and affirmed throughout their various writings.

In 1767 the Wesley brothers published *Hymns on the Trinity,* a substantial collection of hymns designed to combat "the outbreak of Arianism in this country." The hymns on the Trinity were based upon and popularized a scholarly theological text entitled *The Catholic Doctrine of the Trinity Proved By Above a Hundred Short And Clear Arguments in terms of Holy Scripture, Compared In A Manner Entirely New,* published by Rev. William Jones in 1754. The Wesleys' publication followed the format provided by that of Rev. Jones, and hence was divided into four subsections: "The Divinity of Christ," "The Deity and Personality of the Holy Ghost," "Objections Usually Brought to Disguise and Destroy the Scriptural Evidence of This Doctrine," and "the passages of Scripture have been laid together, and made to unite their beams in one common centre, the Unity of the Trinity, which unity is not metaphorical, and figurative, but strict and real." For the section on "The Divinity of Christ," Charles wrote fifty-seven original hymns that explored various biblical passages stressing the full divinity of Jesus Christ and his equality with the Father and the Holy Spirit. As Charles wrote in hymn No. 52, "Thee, O Christ, of God the Son,/In essence, substance, nature One,/Thy Father's equal we proclaim/With God eternally the same." Where contemporary Arians and Socinians doubted the full divinity of Jesus, Charles and John affirmed: "True, absolute Divinity,/Jesus, we dare ascribe to Thee." This affirmation, they believed, was true because it was "grounded on [God's] written word":

> But grounded on Thy written word,
> We worship our almighty Lord:
> In Thee, whom Thy own Spirit reveals,
> The fullness of the Godhead dwells:
> Thy person really Divine,
> Thy body is Jehovah's shrine,
> The whole substantial Deity
> Resides eternally in Thee.

Like John's article of faith, Charles's hymns affirmed the full humanity and full divinity of Jesus Christ. Many of his hymns, like this one based on 2 Corinthians 5:19, "God was in Christ reconciling the world to himself," assigned the humanity of Jesus the role of substitute for sinful humanity on the cross, and gave Jesus' divinity the role of redemption itself. Charles described Jesus Christ as both "Patient" and "Agent" of our reconciliation:

> 1. God was in Christ, th' eternal Sire
>   Reveal'd in His eternal Son,
>   Jehovah did on earth expire,
>   For every soul of man t' atone:
>   The one mighty God supreme,
>   Jehovah lavish of His blood
>   Pour'd out th' inestimable stream,
>   And reconcil'd the world to God.
>
> 2. The one, true, the only God most high,
>   Agent at once and Patient was:
>   As Man He did for sinners die,
>   As God redeem'd us by His cross;
>   Jesus the general debt hath paid,
>   God in the person of the Son
>   Amends to God the Father made,
>   For Son and Father are but one.

The Incarnation

"Why did God become man?" was the famous question raised and addressed by Anselm of Canterbury (1033-1109) in his tome by that title *(Cur Deus Homo?)*. In his work Anselm stressed that God became human in order to save humans from sin and death; in so doing, Anselm pioneered the so-called "satisfaction theory" of the atonement. John Deschner suggests that John Wesley sought to answer this same question of why God became man over against the larger context of his disagreement with staunch Calvinists on the matter of predestination. In this context, one answer to the question is simply: "because God decreed it from all eternity."

If we press the question further, as to the reason God decreed the incarnation, Wesley's solution points both to God's love and God's justice. John describes God's love as "His darling, His reigning attribute which sheds an amiable glory on all His other perfections." And yet God's justice must also be taken into account: "even that vindictive justice whose essential character and principal office is, to punish sin, and which must be preserved inviolate." Thus, John believed that because of God's love, God determined from all eternity that he would save sinful humans by becoming one of them and paying the price of their sins; in this Wesley follows Anselm, but without Anselm's emphasis upon "satisfaction."

In their sermon No. 146, "The One Thing Needful," which John wrote and both brothers preached, the Wesleys gave a more characteristic and distinctive rationale for the incarnation, and indeed for the entire Christ-event: "May not the same truth appear . . . that this was the one end of our redemption; of all our blessed Lord did and suffered for us; of his incarnation, his life, his death? All these miracles of love were wrought with no other view than to restore us to health and freedom." In their emphasis upon the incarnation, life, and death of Jesus Christ restoring humanity to "health and freedom" the Wesleys followed a pattern reminiscent of the ancient Eastern Church Fathers, such as Irenaeus (ca. 125-202), who wrote: "He [Christ] became what we are to make us what He is." In this sense, sanctification and human restoration to wholeness ("the one thing needful") is the chief aim of the Christ-event.

This same soteriological emphasis is maintained throughout Charles Wesley's hymns. These familiar lines from his "Hymn for Christmas Day" make this point as well as any:

3. Christ, by highest heaven adored,
   Christ, the everlasting Lord,
   Late in time behold Him come,
   Offspring of a virgin's womb.

4. Veil'd in flesh, the Godhead see,
   Hail th' incarnate Deity!
   Pleased as man with men t' appear
   Jesus, our Immanuel here!

5. Hail the heavenly Prince of Peace!
   Hail the Sun of Righteousness!
   Light and life to all He brings,
   Risen with healing in His wings.

In these verses by the younger Wesley, we can observe the same emphases upon incarnation and sanctification — as healing — that we saw in "The One Thing Needful." The Incarnate One not only comes to redeem fallen humanity from sin and death; he has become "man with men" to bring "healing in His wings" and thereby to mend our brokenness.

Prophet, Priest, and King

The Protestant Reformers, notably John Calvin in his famous *Institutes of the Christian Religion* (1559), used the threefold formula "Prophet, Priest, and King" to summarize the person and saving work of Jesus Christ. In his "Letter to a Roman Catholic" John Wesley delineated his own Christology by using the threefold office, and also explained how he understood it:

> I believe that Jesus of Nazareth was the Saviour of the world, the Messiah so long foretold, that being anointed with the Holy Ghost,
> He was a *prophet* revealing to us the whole will of God;
> That he was a *priest,* who gave himself [as] a sacrifice for sin, and still makes intercession for transgressors;
> That he is a *king,* who has all power in heaven and earth, and will reign till he has subdued all things unto himself.

In John's sermon "The Law Established through Faith, Discourse II," he explained what it means to properly preach Christ by using the threefold office:

> To preach Christ as a workman that needeth not be ashamed [2 Tim. 2:15] is to preach him not only as our great "*High Priest,* taken from among men, and ordained for men, in things pertaining to God" [Heb. 5:1], as such, "reconciling us to God by his blood" [Rom. 5:9, 10], and "ever living to make intercession for us" [Heb. 7:25] but likewise as the *Prophet of the Lord,* "who of God is made unto wisdom" [1 Cor. 1:30], who by his word and his Spirit "is with us always" [Matt. 28:20], "guiding us into all truth" [John 16:13], yea, as remaining a *King forever* as giving laws to all whom he has bought with his blood; as restoring those to the image of God whom he had first reinstated in his favor; as reigning in all believing hearts until he has "subdued all things to himself" [Phil. 3:21]; until he hath utterly cast out all sin, and "brought in everlasting righteousness" [Dan. 9:24].

Charles's hymns employ the threefold office in similar fashion. The following hymn, from *Hymns and Sacred Poems* (1739), where it is entitled "Hymn to the Son," illustrates this point quite well:

6. Prophet, to me reveal
   Thy Father's perfect will;
   Never mortal spake like thee,
   Human prophet like divine;
   Loud and strong their voices be,
   Small, and still, and inward thine!

7. On thee, my Priest, I call;
   Thy blood atoned for all.
   Still the Lamb as slain appears;
   Still thou stand'st before the throne,
   Ever off'ring up my prayers,
   These presenting with thy own.

8. Jesu, thou art my King,
   From thee my strength I bring:
   Shadowed by thy mighty hand,

Saviour, who shall pluck me thence?
Faith supports, by faith I stand,
Strong as thy omnipotence.

While Charles's hymns employ the threefold office with surprising frequency, many of his lyrics show a marked preference for the priestly office of Jesus Christ — in which the Savior is both high priest and sacrificial victim, who intercedes for sinners with his own blood.

Imputed Righteousness

John Wesley's sermon No. 20, "The Lord Our Righteousness," was written during the Wesleys' ongoing controversy with staunch Calvinists both within and outside of the Methodist movement. Calvinists charged the Wesleys with teaching "works righteousness" because they persisted in maintaining the Anglican balance between saving faith and the importance of doing good works. The Wesleys, for their part, charged the Calvinists with antinomianism — the notion that good works were an indifferent matter to the person who had received saving faith. In "The Lord Our Righteousness" John sought to demonstrate that he wholeheartedly affirmed the Reformation doctrine of imputed righteousness even while he made room for a righteousness that grows within a Christian's life as a saving faith is exercised in doing good works.

In a way, the discussion about "The Lord Our Righteousness" boiled down to a choice between "imputed righteousness," which describes the saving righteousness of Christ that is given to the believer by faith, and "imparted righteousness," which describes the way actual righteousness grows in the believer's life in doing good works. Stated in biblical terms, it was an argument between St. Paul and St. James; it was in essence a debate between the strict *sola fideism* ("faith only") of Martin Luther and the Anglo-Catholic synthesis of faith and good works. John Wesley's debt to St. Paul and to the Protestant reformers is unmistakable:

> But in what sense is this righteousness imputed to believers? In this: all believers are forgiven and accepted, not for the sake of anything in them, or anything that ever was, that is, or ever can be done by them, but wholly and solely for the sake of what Christ hath done and suffered for them. I say again, not for the sake of anything in them or done by them,

of their own righteousness or works. "Not for works of righteousness which we have done, but of his own mercy he saved us" [Titus 3:5]. "By grace ye are saved through faith. . . . Not of works, lest any man should boast" [Eph. 2:8-9]; but wholly and solely for the sake of what Christ hath done and suffered for us. . . . And this is not only the means of our *obtaining* the favour of God, but of our continuing therein.

Yet John also owed a debt to St. James and to the Anglo-Catholic tradition, so he attempted to steer a middle course between the two extreme alternatives. Having strongly affirmed *imputed* righteousness, which is received by faith in Christ alone, he turned to discuss in what sense it can properly be said that righteousness is also *implanted* and operative in believers. Hence, John replied to his critics: " 'But do not you believe *inherent* righteousness?' Yes, in its proper place; not as the *ground* of our acceptance with God, but as the *fruit* of it; not in the place of *imputed* righteousness, but as consequent upon it. That is, I believe God *implants* righteousness in every one to whom he has *imputed* it."

Going on to give this consequent, implanted righteousness a Christological and soteriological focus, Wesley wrote: "I believe 'Jesus Christ is made of God unto us sanctification' [1 Cor. 1:30], as well as righteousness; or that God sanctifies, as well as justifies, all them that believe in him. They to whom the righteousness of Christ is imputed are made righteous by the Spirit of Christ, are renewed in the image of God 'after the likeness wherein they were created, in righteousness and true holiness' [Eph. 4:24]." Thus the Wesleys pursued a "middle way" between the *sola fideism* of the Protestant Reformation, with its accompanying danger of antinomianism, and the imparted righteousness of the Anglo-Catholic tradition, with its accompanying danger of works righteousness.

The Imitation of Christ

Over the course of his long life John Wesley published seven editions of *The Imitation of Christ* by Thomas à Kempis (ca. 1380-1471). The literary work, which John often called "The Christian Pattern," as well as the theme it stressed had a profound effect upon him during his college years. In 1729 it was one of the works that caused him to recognize "the indispensable necessity of having the mind which was in Christ, and of walking as Christ also walked . . . in all things." The book became a part of the steady diet of the Oxford Holy Club, and it was one of the few books John took along on his missionary stint in Georgia. Even though it does not emerge as a prominent theme in their published sermons, "imitating Christ" was a constant focus for both Wesleys. And their "Large Minutes" of 1763, which was published as a summary of the minutes of the previous annual conferences, insisted that a copy of "Kempis" should be found in every Methodist society and every Christian home. As Geordan Hammond points out, "The dictim 'having the mind of Christ and walking as he walked,' a combination of Philippians 2:5 and 1 John 2:6, is the most frequently found biblical expression in [John's] sermons with over fifty occurrences." Thus, he rightly concludes that "A burning zeal to imitate Christ was a defining characteristic of his early life and lifetime of ministry."

Receiving Christ

The Wesleys embraced classical Christian views on the person and work of Jesus Christ, differing from the church fathers and the ancient creeds only on the matter of Christ's reputed descent into hell, which John Wesley did not find to be taught in the New Testament. His "note" on Acts 2:27 makes this clear: "It doth not appear that ever our Lord went to hell. His soul, when it separated from the body, did not go thither, but to paradise, Luke 22:43."

More important than affirming the classical verities about Jesus Christ, however, was the event of receiving Christ by faith. John's sermon "The Catholic Spirit" contained a series of pointed scriptural questions designed to lead the hearer to the reception of Christ by faith. Once again the soteriological focus of the Wesleys' Christology is well displayed in these questions that are intended to prepare a person to "receive Christ":

> Dost thou believe in the Lord Jesus Christ, "God over all, blessed forever" [2 Cor. 5:7]?
> Is he "revealed in thy soul" [Gal. 1:16]?
> Dost thou "know Jesus Christ and him crucified" [Rom. 9:5]?
> Does he "dwell in thee, and thou in him" [John 6:56; 1 John 4:13, 15]?
> Is he "formed in thy heart by faith" [Gal. 4:19]?
> Having absolutely disclaimed all thy own works, thy own righteousness, hast thou "submitted thyself unto the righteousness of God," "which is by faith in Christ Jesus" [Rom. 3:22]?

Art thou "found in him, not having thy own righteousness, but the righteousness which is by faith" [Phil. 3:9]?

And art thou, through him, "fighting the good fight of faith, and laying hold of eternal life" [1 Tim. 6:12]?

QUESTIONS FOR REFLECTION

1. To what degree does "having the mind of Christ and walking as he walked" shape your own Christian faith?
2. Is your view of Jesus Christ (Christology) profoundly connected to your understanding of Christian salvation (soteriology)?
3. Have you "received" the atonement? Have you "received" Christ?
4. How do you understand the threefold office of Jesus Christ: Prophet, Priest, and King?
5. How do you understand the "person of Christ"? The "work of Christ"?

SUGGESTIONS FOR FURTHER READING

Deschner, John. *Wesley's Christology: An Interpretation* (Dallas: SMU Press, 1985).

Riss, Richard M. "John Wesley's Christology in Recent Literature," *The Wesleyan Theological Journal* 45:1 (Spring 2010): 108-29.

Rattenbury, J. Ernest. *The Evangelical Doctrines of Charles Wesley's Hymns* (London: Epworth Press, 1941), chapters 8, 11.

Wesley, John. Standard Sermon No. 20, "The Lord Our Righteousness."

CHAPTER EIGHT

He Breaks the Power of Canceled Sin

....

CHRISTIAN PERFECTION

I am glad that Brother D— has more light with regard to full sanctification. This doctrine is the grand *depositum* which God had lodged with the people called Methodists, and for the sake of propagating this chiefly he appeared to have raised us up.

John Wesley, Letter, September 15, 1790

"Full sanctification," "entire sanctification," "perfect love," and "Christian Perfection" were and are all synonyms in Wesleyan theological parlance. In the quotation above, John Wesley registers his conviction that it was chiefly for the promulgation of this doctrine that the Methodists were providentially raised up by God. None of the phrases that the Wesleys used to describe the upper reaches of Christian holiness were common to the Protestant Reformers. Albert Outler rightly described Christian Perfection as both "the most distinctive and also the most widely misunderstood of all Wesley's doctrines":

Protestants, convinced of the *simul justus et peccator*[1] — and used to translating *perfecto* as some sort of perfected perfection — were bound to see in the Wesleyan doctrine, despite all its formal disclaimers, a bald advertisement of spiritual pride and implicitly, works-righteousness. Even the Methodists, working from their own unexamined Latin traditions of forensic righteousness, tended to interpret "perfection" in terms of a spiritual elitism — and so misunderstood Wesley and the early Eastern

1. "Simultaneously just and yet a sinner" (Latin), in Martin Luther's famous dictum.

traditions of *teleiosas* [Greek: perfect, complete, whole, or mature] as a never-ending inspiration for all love's fullness (perfecting perfection).

John Wesley recognized the difficulty of this theological language for those who were not enamored with the early Greek Church Fathers and the English holy-living tradition to the degree that he and his brother Charles were. In his 1741 sermon entitled "Christian Perfection," based on Philippians 3:12, John averred, "There is scarce any expression in Holy Writ which has given more offense than this. The word 'perfect' is what many cannot bear. The very sound of it is an abomination to them. And whosoever 'preaches perfection' (as the phrase is), i.e. asserts that it is attainable in this life, runs great hazard of being accounted by them worse than a heathen man or a publican."

John Wesley knew full well the extent of the offense, because that particular sermon was written in the aftermath of a soul-straining interview with his own resident Anglican Bishop, the Rev. Edmund Gibson, late in 1740. Gibson felt some responsibility for oversight of the Methodist movement, since the movement was headquartered in London, in Gibson's diocese. Bishop Gibson wanted a direct account from Wesley of this "new doctrine" he was preaching all over his jurisdiction. John explained, "I told him, without any disguise or reserve. When I had ceased speaking, he said, 'Mr. Wesley, if this be all you mean, publish it to all the world. If anyone then can confute what you say, he may have free leave.' I answered, 'My Lord, I will.'" A part of John's response was his written and published sermon, "Christian Perfection," which he also preached in 1741.

In the introduction to "Christian Perfection," John acknowledged that "some have advised, wholly to lay aside the use of these expressions, 'because they have given so great offense.' But are they not found in the oracles of God? If so, by what authority can any messenger of God lay them aside, even though all men should be offended? . . . Whatsoever God hath spoken, that will we speak, whether men will hear or whether they will forebear: knowing that then alone can any minister of Christ be 'pure from the blood of all men,' when he hath 'not shunned to declare unto them all the counsel of God' [Acts 20:26-27]." The Wesleys used "Christian Perfection" and "entire sanctification" as terms to describe the upper reaches of Christian holiness, a constant state of Christian maturity, free from willful and intentional sin.[2]

---

2. The Wesleys' definition of "sin properly so called," as a "willful violation of a known law of God," plays a very foundational role in this formulation, since it causes them to speak of perfection as a matter of heart and will.

Consistency was a point of pride with John Wesley, and he was concerned both to explain his doctrine of "Christian Perfection" and prove that he and Charles had taught what was essentially the same doctrine over the whole span of their highly productive ministries. John's *magnum opus* on this topic, *A Plain Account of Christian Perfection As Believed and Taught by the Reverend Mr. John Wesley from the Year 1725 to the Year 1777*, was his main and perhaps most definitive summary. Surprisingly, John takes his reader back beyond his conversion experience of May 1738 to the year 1725, as he explains how he came to formulate his doctrine of Christian Perfection. What the Wesleys learned through their conversion experiences of 1738 was the importance of justification by faith and Christian assurance; they had their doctrine of holiness well in hand by then. They simply needed to reorder their understanding of holiness in concert with their newly found realization of saving faith and assurance of salvation.

In 1725, at the age of twenty-three, John Wesley — the "Oxford Methodist" — read Bishop Jeremy Taylor's *Rules and Exercises of Holy Living and Dying*. He reported being "exceedingly affected" by it. "Instantly I resolved," he wrote, "to dedicate all my life to God, all my thoughts and words, and actions; being thoroughly convinced there was no medium; but that every part of my life (not some only) must either be a sacrifice to God, or myself, that is, in effect, to the devil." The next year, John read *The Imitation of Christ* by Thomas à Kempis. This work taught John Wesley "that 'simplicity of intention, and purity of affection, one design in all we speak or do, and one desire ruling all our tempers,' are indeed 'the wings of the soul,' without which she can never ascend to the mount of God." By 1729, John reported that he was seeking and finding these same salient themes in the Bible — "which he began not only to read, but to study" as "the one, the only standard of truth, and the only model of pure religion." This caused him to see "in a clearer and clearer light, the indispensable necessity of having 'the mind which was in Christ,' and of 'walking as Christ also walked'; even of having, not some part only, but all the mind which was in Him; and of walking as He walked, not only in many or in most respects, but in all things. And this was the light, wherein at this time I generally considered religion, as a uniform following of Christ, an entire inward and outward conformity to our Master."

As evidence of this deepening emphasis John pointed to his Oxford-era sermon "Circumcision of the Heart" (1733), in which he described holiness in this manner: "It is that habitual disposition of soul which, in the Sacred Writings, is termed 'holiness,' and which directly implies the being cleansed from sin, 'from all filthiness both of flesh and spirit,' and, by consequence, the being endued with those virtues which were in Christ Jesus, the being so 'renewed in the image of our mind' [Rom. 12:1] as to be 'perfect, as our Father in heaven is perfect' [Matt. 5:8]." At this same time John began to see that "Love is the fulfilling of the law, the end of the commandment. It is not only 'the first and great' command, but all the commandments in one." Hence, in that pre-conversion sermon, John urged himself and others: "Let your soul be filled with so entire a love to God, that you may love nothing but for His sake. Have a pure intention of heart, a steadfast regard to His glory in all our actions. For then, and not till then, is that mind in us, which was also in Christ Jesus when every motion of our heart, in every word of our tongue, in every work of our hands, we pursue nothing but in relation to Him, and in subordination to His pleasure." As John returned from Georgia in spring 1738, he described "the cry of his heart" by using these lines from one of his early hymns:

> O grant that nothing in my soul
> > May dwell, but Thy pure love alone!
> O may Thy love possess me whole,
> > My joy, my treasure, and my crown,
> Strange fires far from my heart remove —
> My every act, word, thought, be love!

After their conversions in May 1738, John and Charles continued to affirm entire sanctification or Christian Perfection, but now they located it *after* the event of receiving God's acceptance (justification by faith), instead of thinking of it as a basis *for* receiving God's approval. The "New Birth," as we saw in a previous chapter, which was described as "initial sanctification," begins a long process of transformation through "works of piety and works of mercy" whereby we become more and more conformed to the image of God in which we were originally created (Gen. 1:26).

Although it was preceded by the published sermon "Christian Perfection," John Wesley called "The Character of a Methodist" (1742) "the first tract I ever wrote expressly on this subject." In "The Character of a Methodist," John described the grand *depositum*:

> A Methodist is one who loves the Lord his God with all his heart, with all his soul, with all his mind, and with all his strength. God is the joy of

his heart, and the desire of his soul, which is continually crying "whom have I in heaven but Thee?" and "there is none upon earth whom I desire besides Thee." My God and my all! "Thou are the strength of my heart, and my portion forever." He is therefore happy in God; yea, always happy, as having in him a well of water springing up into everlasting life and overflowing his soul with peace and joy. Perfect love having now cast out fear, he rejoices evermore. . . . For he is "pure in heart." Love has purified his heart from envy, malice, wrath, and every unkind temper.

Albert Outler pointed out that in describing a Methodist in such elevated terms, John Wesley actually borrowed Clement of Alexandria's (ca. 150-215) concept of the "Perfect Christian." It was an old idea for a new age.

A Definition of Perfection

In several of his works John Wesley began his definition of Christian Perfection by explaining in what sense those who experienced Christian Perfection were *not* perfect. This was an obvious attempt to answer detractors, but it also put the Wesleys in the awkward position of seeming to teach a sort of "imperfect perfection." But the tension between their willingness to use the extravagant term "perfection" on the one hand, and their embrace of the godly humility of Philippians 3:12 ("Not as though I had already attained, either were already perfect") on the other means that it is probably better to describe this phenomenon as "perfecting perfection," an ongoing process of transformation, rather than "imperfect perfection," which sounds more like an utter contradiction in terms.

In his tract "Thoughts on Christian Perfection" (1759) John responded to the rhetorical question "What is Christian Perfection?" by affirming "loving God with all our heart, mind, soul, and strength. This implies that no wrong temper, none contrary to love, remains in the soul; and that all the thoughts, words, and actions are governed by pure love." Responding to a second rhetorical question — "Do you affirm that this perfection excludes all infirmities, ignorance and mistakes?" — John explained, "I continually affirm quite the contrary, and always have done so." In response to a third question — "But how can every thought, word, and work, be governed by pure love, and the man be subject, at the same time, to ignorance and mistake?" — he continued:

I see no contradiction here: "A man may be filled with pure love, and still be liable to mistake." Indeed, I do not expect to be freed from actual mistakes, till this mortal puts on immortality. I believe this to be a natural consequence of the soul's dwelling in flesh and blood. For we cannot now think at all, but by the mediation of those bodily organs which have suffered equally with the rest of our frame. And hence we cannot avoid sometimes thinking wrong, till this corruptible shall have put on incorruption [1 Cor. 15:50].

So for John Wesley, Christian Perfection does *not* imply being made free from the physical and mental limitations associated with life in a moral, fallen body. What is being "perfected" or is "being made perfect in love" is our will, and our attitudes, which are being transformed by God's love working within us, so that we are able to love God with all our heart, soul, strength, and mind, and to love our neighbor as ourselves. Christian Perfection, in this sense, means whole-hearted consecration to God, as opposed to the opposite — being a "double-minded" person (James 1:5).

One of John Wesley's last major forays into the topic of Christian Perfection was his sermon No. 77, which Wesley wrote towards the end of his career (1784), and published in his *Arminian Magazine* in 1785. Working from Hebrews 6:1, "Let us go on to perfection," Wesley again first explained in what sense mature Christians are *not* perfect:

The highest perfection which man can attain while the soul dwells in the body does not exclude ignorance and error, and a thousand other infirmities. Now from wrong judgments wrong words and actions will often necessarily flow. And in some cases wrong affections also may spring from the same source. I may judge wrong of *you;* I may think more or less highly of you than I ought to think. And this mistake in my judgment may not only occasion something wrong in my behavior, but it may have a still deeper effect — it may occasion something wrong in my affection. From a wrong apprehension I may love and esteem you either more or less than I ought. Nor can I be freed from a liableness to such a mistake while I remain in a corruptible body. A thousand infirmities in consequence of this will attend my spirit till it returns to God who gave it. And in numberless instances it comes short of doing the will of God as Adam did in paradise.

Here John comes very close to using the classical (forensic) definition of sin ("that which comes short of doing the will of God") to describe what he means by mistakes and liability to corruption. This should remind us that when Wesley is concerning himself with sin in believers, his attention is focused not upon the corruption of our physical self (which we cannot do anything about), but rather upon our inner state (heart, mind, soul) which is being renewed by the purifying power of God's love. The Christian Perfection that Wesley envisions for Christian believers, then, allows that they can be free from sin "properly so-called"; that is, from "willful violations of a known law of God." This sort of "perfecting perfection" describes how the human will is being transformed by a constant infusion of God's love:

> What is then the perfection of which man is capable while he dwells in a corruptible body? It is the complying with that kind command, "My son, give me thy heart" [Prov. 23:26]. It is the "loving the Lord his God, with all his heart, and with all his soul, and with all his mind" [Matt. 22:37f]. This is the sum of Christian Perfection: it is all comprised in that one word, love. The first branch of it is the love of God, and as he that loves God loves his brother also [1 John 4:21], it is inseparably connected with the second, "Thou shalt love thy neighbour as thyself" [Lev. 19:18, Matt. 19:19]. Thou shalt love every man as thy own soul, as Christ loved us. "On these two commandments hang all the law and the prophets" [Matt. 22:40]: these contain the whole of Christian perfection.

John Wesley was able to point to many lines in Charles's hymns that paralleled and reinforced his own understanding of Christian perfection. One such example, from Charles Wesley's *Hymns and Sacred Poems,* 1749 edition, which John did not see prior to their publication, illustrates what the elder Wesley pointed to in his *Plain Account of Christian Perfection:*

> Turn me, Lord, and turn me now;
> To Thy yoke my spirit bow;
> Grant me now the pearl to find
> Of a meek and quiet mind.

> Calm, O calm my troubled breast;
> Let me gain that second rest;
> From my works for ever cease;
> Perfected in holiness.

The conclusion which John Wesley gave at the end of his survey of Charles's hymns is a good barometer of what John and Charles thought about Christian perfection at that time:

> I have been the more large in these extracts [samples from Charles's 1749 hymns] because, hence it appears beyond all possibility of exception that to this day, both my brother and I maintained: (1) That Christian perfection is that love of God and neighbour, which implies deliverance from all sin. (2) That this is received merely by faith. (3) That it is given instantaneously, in one moment. (4) That we are to expect it, not at death, but every moment; that now is the accepted time, now is the day of this salvation.

A Brotherly Debate

The mid-1760s saw several events that proved to be decisive for John and Charles Wesley's understanding of Christian Perfection. One of those developments was the fact that two of the Wesleys' lay preachers in London, Thomas Maxfield and George Bell, fell into religious fanaticism. They began to predict the imminent end of the world, and to preach that Christian believers could be made "as perfect as angels" by simply claiming perfection as an act of faith. The negative fallout from this was so severe that John Wesley reported: "They made the very name of Perfection stink in the nostrils of those who loved and honored it before." And one of the people who seemed to have been adversely affected by the fanatical claimants of Christian Perfection was Charles Wesley.

Charles's *Short Hymns on Select Passages of Scripture,* published in 1762, evidences some of his hostility toward fanatical claims of Christian Perfection. In his preface to the *Short Hymns* Charles wrote: "Several of the hymns are intended to prove, and several to guard, the doctrine of Christian Perfection. I durst not publish one without the other." He continued, "I use some severity; not against particular persons, but against Enthusiasts and Antinomianians, who by not living up to their profession [of this doctrine] . . . cause the truth to be evil spoken of."

While Charles's hymns held out the possibility of receiving Christian Perfection in this life, he became increasingly critical of those (like Bell and Maxfield) who actually claimed to have received that blessing. His concept, like John's, was a perfecting perfection which was a process of inner purification. Hence, in 1762, in his poetical comment on Matthew 5:48 ("Be ye perfect"), Charles wrote:

1. Wouldst Thou require what cannot be?
    The thing impossible to me
   Is possible with God:
    I trust Thy truth to make me just,
   Th' omnipotence of love I trust,
    The virtue of Thy blood.

But for Charles, the realization of utter perfection seemed to be increasingly impossible to grasp — hoped for, and yearned for, but not something one could hastily "snatch," as some of the fanatics seemed to imply:

3. Thou waitest still, when Thee I know,
    A larger blessing to bestow,
   A second gift impart,
    (The sinless mind, the farther rest,)
   And stamp Thine image on my breast,
    And fill my emptied heart.

4. Yet till Thy time is fully come,
    I dare not hastily presume*
   To snatch the perfect grace.
    But humbly patient to the end,
   And praying at Thy feet attend,
    Till Thou unveil thy face.

At the point of the asterisk, John Wesley, operating as Charles's editor (after publication of these hymns) wrote a retort: "I dare say NOW is the accepted time!" John did not approve of Charles's increasing tendency to see Christian Perfection as something that occurred at "the end" — as the believer laid the corruptible body down in death. Yet Charles continued to disagree. He wrote a poem based on Matthew 20:22 ("Ye know not what ye ask"):

1. Advancement in Thy kingdom here
    Whoe'er impatiently desire,
   They know not, Lord, the pangs severe,

> The trials which they first require;
> They all must first Thy sufferings share,
>   Ambitious of their calling's prize,
> And every day Thy burden bear,
>   And thus to *late* perfection rise.

2. Nature would fain evade, or flee
     That sad necessity of pain;
   But who refuse to die with Thee,
     With Thee shall never, never reign:
   The sorrow doth the joy ensure,
     The crown for conquerors prepared;
   And all who to the end endure,
     Shall grasp through death the full reward.*

At the asterisk, John Wesley's editorial pen wrote: "Not until Death?"

A second growing disagreement between John and Charles, related to Christian Perfection, was whether entire sanctification could occur "in a moment" or whether it was more likely the result of a long pilgrimage toward mature Christian faith. Earlier on, there was no disagreement. Among Charles's hymns of the 1740s, for example, were these lines:

> Lay but Thine hand upon my soul,
> And *instantaneously* made whole
>   My soul by faith shall rise,
> Shall rise by faith and upright stand,
> And answer all Thy just command
>   In all its faculties.

But by the time Charles was writing his *Short Hymns on Select Passages of Scripture* (1762), he had come to see Christian Perfection as more of a gradual, transforming event. In fact, "gradual holiness" was becoming one of his standard phrases. Commenting upon Genesis 2:1, for example, Charles wrote:

> Who madest thus the earth and skies,
>   A world, a six days' work of Thine,
> Thou bidd'st the new creation rise,
>   Nobler effect of grace Divine!

We might spring up at Thy command,
    For glory in an instant meet;
But by Thy will at last we stand
    In *gradual holiness* complete.

A third area of tension between John and Charles Wesley over the doctrine of Christian Perfection emerged through an ongoing discussion about human "sinlessness" as it related to entire sanctification. Many of the hymns in their early ministry celebrate salvation as joyous victory over both the guilt and power of sin. For example, Charles's well-known conversion hymn, "O for a Thousand Tongues to Sing," arguably his most famous hymn, proclaims: "He breaks the power of cancell'd sin,/He sets the prisoner free." The Wesleys' poetical "Prayer Against the Power of Sin" concluded on a similar note: "I shall sin no more!" Charles's *Hymns and Sacred Poems,* 1749 edition, evidence these same sentiments in a whole section of hymns entitled "Waiting for Full Redemption"; these hymns voiced the affirmation that redemption is "full" — that is to say, entire and not partial — and that the singer was still "waiting" for it to arrive.

But by 1766 John wrote a pointed letter to his brother in which he warned Charles about setting perfection "so high": "There is no such perfection here as you describe it — at least, I never met an instance of it; and I doubt I ever shall. Therefore, I still think to set perfection so high is effectually to renounce it." Charles apparently had moved more and more toward preaching Christian perfection as an utter ideal, which provided direction and power for living a life of discipleship, but which was not realized until the body was laid down in death. But an unqualified conception of perfection, if married to John's rhetoric about receiving perfection as an instantaneous gift of God's grace, could lead to disastrous results — as the fanatical perfectionists had clearly illustrated.

Additionally, more often than John, Charles drew a direct line of connection between suffering and Christian perfection. This was particularly true of Charles's later hymns, written in a forced retirement from active ministerial life due to ill health. This development was evidenced by the sad-sounding "Preface" to his *Short Hymns* (1762): "God, having graciously laid His hand upon my body, and disabled me for the principal work of the ministry, has thereby given me an unexpected occasion of writing the following hymns." According to Frank Baker, among Charles's many physical ailments were "pleurisy, neuralgia, lumbago, dysentery, piles, rheumatism, gout, and scurvys." A melancholy of the soul often accompanied these physical ailments, and so in an autobiographical-sounding hymn on Genesis 49:18 ("I have awaited Thy salvation"), Charles described his life as coming to an end after three-score years of waiting for full salvation ("perfect righteousness" and "pure of heart") within "the vale of tears":

> Jesus, throughout my threescore years
>   I have for Thy salvation stay'd,
> And leaving now the vale of tears,
>   I dare not doubt Thy promised aid;
> Kept by Thy power from acting sin,
>   The end of Thy power I here shall see,
> Thy perfect righteousness brought in,
>   And pure of heart return to Thee.

Charles seemed to have come to the conclusion that suffering had purifying effects upon the human soul. This was particularly evident in his poetical comments on the Book of Job, where he described the "sanctified use of woe" by suggesting that through suffering the Christian can be purified and thereby prepared for heavenly glory. This emphasis often merged with others mentioned earlier, in which an unqualified conception of entire sanctification was realized through suffering, in the "article of death":

> Better for me to live, if Thou
>   My tempted soul with strength supply,
> And *then* my hoary head to bow,
>   And perfected through sufferings, die.

An Eleven-Point Plan

At the very end of his *Plain Account of Christian Perfection,* John Wesley offered an eleven-point summary of Christian perfection as he understood, taught, and preached it. These eleven points, upon which he thought there was complete agreement among the early Methodists, were as follows:

1. There is such a thing as perfection; for it is again and again mentioned in the Scriptures.
2. It is not so early as justification; for justified persons are to "go on to perfection" (Heb. 6:1).

3. It is not so late as death; for St. Paul speaks of living men that were perfect (Phil. 3:13).

4. It is not absolute. Absolute perfection belongs not to man, nor to angels, but to God alone.

5. It does not make any man infallible; none is infallible, while he remains in the body.

6. Is it sinless? It is not worth while to contend for the term. It is "salvation from sin."

7. It is "perfect love" (1 John 4:18). This is the essence of it; its properties, inseparable fruits, are rejoicing evermore, praying without ceasing, and in everything giving thanks (1 Thess. 5:16).

8. It is improvable. It is so far from lying in an indivisible point, from being incapable of increase, that one perfected in love may grow in grace far swifter than he did before.

9. It is amissable, capable of being lost; of which we have numerous instances. But we were not thoroughly convinced of this, till five or six years ago.

10. It is constantly both preceded and followed by a gradual work [of grace].

11. But is it in itself instantaneous or not? . . . An instantaneous change has been wrought in some believers. None can deny this. . . . But in some, this change was not instantaneous. They did not perceive the instant when it was wrought. It is often [for example] difficult to perceive the instant when a man dies, yet there is an instant in which life ceases. And if ever sin ceases, there must be a last moment of its existence, and that first moment of our deliverance from it.

John Wesley persistently defined Christian perfection in terms of loving God with all one's heart, mind, and strength, and loving one's neighbor as oneself (Matt. 22:37-39). This purity of intention is a consistent Christian maturity ("perfection," or "wholeness"), which fulfills God's law through love and does not willfully violate a known law of God. Intentional sin ceases to dominate and determine our lives as we are being filled and transformed by God's love. This was an entire sanctification for which the Wesleys longed, in which inbred sin was purged out by the Holy Spirit and attitudes and actions were healed and renewed. Charles sang about this "perfect holiness and love" in a "Short Hymn" on Psalm 103:3 that was reprinted in John's "big" 1780 hymnal:

1. What! Never speak one evil word!
    Or rash, or idle or unkind?

O how shall I, most gracious Lord,
   This mark of true perfection find?

2. Thy sinless mind in me reveal,
   Thy Spirit's plenitude impart,
And all my spotless life shall tell
   Th'abundance of thy loving heart.

3. Saviour, I long to testify
   The fullness of thy gracious power;
O might thy Spirit the blood apply
   Which bought for me the peace — and more!

4. Forgive, and make my nature whole,
   My inbred malady remove;
To perfect health restore my soul,
   To perfect holiness and love.

QUESTIONS FOR FURTHER REVIEW

1. How would you describe entire sanctification or Christian Perfection?
2. Why did John Wesley consider this doctrine to be "the grand *depositum*" of Methodism?
3. What do you think are the relative strengths and weaknesses of the Wesleys' doctrine of Christian Perfection?
4. Do you agree with John or Charles relative to the "brotherly debate" over the timing, extent, and nature of Christian perfection? Is it instantaneous or gradual? Is it received in death or at any time? Is it qualified or unqualified?

FOR FURTHER READING

Lindstrom, Harold. *Wesley and Sanctification* (Grand Rapids: Francis Asbury Press/Zondervan, 1980).

Tyson, John R. *Charles Wesley on Sanctification* (Grand Rapids: Francis Asbury Press/Zondervan, 1986).

Wesley, John. *A Plain Account of Christian Perfection.*

CHAPTER NINE

An Interest in My Savior's Blood

THE ATONEMENT

And can it be that I should gain
An interest in the Savior's blood,
Died he for me, who caused his pain?
For me, who him to death pursued?
Amazing love! How can it be,
That thou my God, shouldst die for me?

Charles Wesley, *Hymns & Sacred Poems,* 1739

Atonement theory describes the way in which the saving death of Jesus Christ reconciles fallen humans with God — how the cross of Christ creates "at-one-ment" or reconciliation between sinful humanity and our Holy God. John Wesley opined that the atonement (like original sin) was "properly the distinguishing point between Deism and Christianity." While Deism lacked a doctrine of original sin and looked at Jesus primarily as a great moral teacher who serves as our example, classical Christianity affirmed both a doctrine of original sin and the dual nature of Jesus Christ as both divine and human.

The Wesleys' theology of the atonement is rich and variegated, especially as demonstrated in Charles Wesley's hymns. Randy Maddox sums it up this way: "Wesley's central emphasis about the Atonement was that in Christ the issue of guilt due to our sins has been fully addressed; therefore God can mercifully offer us pardon without violating Divine justice." In their atonement theory, the Wesleys developed a multi-faceted approach, which drew upon the classical options, then blended and expanded them. They drew upon Anslem's satisfaction theory, as well as the sin-as-penalty approach of the Protestant Reformers. This approach merged with a strong emphasis upon the cross as a *victory* over sin and death. Because of the way the Wesleys stressed God's love as both the motive behind and the cleansing power in the atonement, one might also hear a few echoes of Peter Abelard's (1079-1142) love-centered "exemplarist" approach. And, as we noted above, there is in the Wesleys' view a strong similarity to the "therapeutic" approach to the atonement made famous by Irenaeus and the early Eastern Church Fathers, in which Jesus Christ not only saves us from sin and death by enabling God to pardon our trespasses, but also makes us whole ("a new creation") by re-creating the image of God within us and healing the brokenness of the inner person. Charles Wesley frequently employed the parable of the Good Samaritan (Luke 10:30ff.) — both in sermon and in song — to stress that Jesus Christ, like the Good Samaritan, is the "Good Physician" of our soul:

> Saviour of my soul, draw nigh,
>   In mercy haste to me;
> At the point of death I lie,
>   And cannot come to Thee.
> Now Thy kind relief afford,
>   The wine and oil of grace pour in,
> Good Physician, speak the word,
>   And heal my soul of sin. . . .
>
> Perfect then the work begun,
>   And make the sinner whole:
> All Thy will on me be done,
>   My body, spirit, soul.
> Still preserve me safe from harms,
>   And kindly for Thy patient care;
> Take me, Jesu, to Thine arms,
>   And keep me ever there.

Following the text of Romans 5:11, "And not only so, but we also joy in God through our Lord Jesus Christ, by whom we have now received the atonement," the Wesley brothers urged that the atonement of Christ was not only a theological verity and a fact of Christian history, but also something that must be "received" in order for its saving, life-giving, healing effects to become operative in a person's life. What it means to "receive the atonement" they delineated as saving faith, as in John's sermon "Salvation by Faith," where he wrote, "Christian faith is then not only an assent to the whole gospel of Christ, but also a full reliance on the blood of Christ, a trust in the merits of his life, death, and resurrection, a recumbency upon him as our atonement and our life, as *given for us* and *living in us.*"

The Blood of Christ

As we see in John Wesley's quotation directly above, in which he spoke of receiving the atonement as "a full reliance on the blood of Christ," references to Jesus' "blood" as atonement abound in the Wesleys' sermons and hymns. "Blood" is a graphic term which the Wesleys used — in sermon and in song — to describe Jesus' saving death. Yet, as John E. Rattenbury pointed out, "Today the term 'blood,' to some minds, obscures what it symbolizes rather than illuminates it." The term is particularly prominent in Charles Wesley's hymns, and for some people it makes them difficult to use in contemporary worship. Yet here again we meet with the Wesleys' desire to be "Bible Christians." The term "blood" appeared more than 375 times in their Bible, and more than 800 times in Charles's later hymns. Clearly, it was a term that they found meaningful and useful in communicating their theology of the atonement.

"Blood" is a graphic term that keeps the harsh reality of Jesus' death ever before us. The basic meaning of the word in the Bible is "death by violence," and it is often used in the Hebrew Scriptures to refer to sacrificial offerings. Both of these meanings resonate well with the Wesleys' atonement theory, because they viewed Jesus' death as costly and horrible for him, while sacrificial and saving for us. The fact that, in the Wesleys' poetical parlance, "God" rhymes with "blood" made these terms a frequent pairing in Charles's hymns. In the following unpublished hymn, "Jesus' blood" is directly paralleled with "the death of God" — which shows something of the foundational meaning he attached to the phrase "Jesus' blood":

> Thy mercies all our thoughts transcend,
>   The worst Thou canst in Christ forgive
> O let our sins and trouble end,
>   O let our dying nation live,
> Hear the loud cry of Jesus' blood
>   And save us by the death of God.

Both John and Charles Wesley speak of there being "merit" in the blood of Christ. In this concept they are following the atonement theory of St. Anselm, in which the value of Christ's death must offset the weight of the whole world's sin. In the following hymn Charles celebrates the coming of the Holy Spirit into the believer's heart as a sign that the believer has been reconciled to God by the merit of Jesus' death:

> Come, thou all-inspiring Spirit,
>   Into every longing heart!
> Bought for us by Jesu's merit,
>   Now thy blissful self impart;
> Sign our uncontested pardon,
>   Wash us in th'atoning blood!
> Make our hearts a watered garden,
>   Fill our spotless souls with God.

As is often the case in Charles's hymns, several atonement images are woven together in these verses. We see purchase language ("bought"), which is reminiscent of Anselm's approach and New Testament images of manumission (for example, Mark 10:45 — "ransom price"), married to cleansing metaphors ("wash us in th'atoning blood") drawn from rites of sacrifice. In this latter sense, Christ is viewed as "my Priest" whose intercession is his own atoning blood:

> On Thee, my Priest, I call;
> Thy blood atoned for all.
>   Still the Lamb as slain appears;
> Still Thou stand'st before the throne,
>   Ever offering up my prayers,
> These presenting with Thy own.

We get the same sense of this connection when we look at passages like Matthew 26:26, where the wine of communion is described as "the blood of the new covenant which is poured out for many for the forgiveness of sins." In Romans 3:25 believers are said to have propitiation for their sins and redemption through faith in the "blood" of Jesus Christ — that is, through faith in his saving death. In Hebrews the death of Jesus Christ is viewed as a sacrificial offering in which Jesus becomes our High Priest, as well as the sacrificial victim, who atones for our sin by offering his own blood as payment for our transgressions — and that of the whole world. Here the comparison between the Levitical priesthood and the sacrificial intercession of Jesus Christ (cf. Heb. 9, 10) is theologically rich and sustained, and verses like Hebrews 9:13-14 were very evocative and formative for the Wesleys: "For if the blood of bulls and of goats . . . sanctified to the purifying of the flesh: How much more shall the blood of Christ, who through the eternal Spirit offered himself without spot to God, purge your conscience from dead works to serve the living God." Not only does Christ, our High Priest, intercede with God on our behalf; Christ also "sprinkles" — and thereby cleanses and redeems us with his blood:

> I now in Christ redemption have,
> I feel it through the sprinkled blood,
>   And testify His power to save,
> And claim Him for my Lord, my God!

In this same connection, Jesus' blood is also said to "wash" or "cleanse" us from our sins. Several New Testament passages, such as 1 John 1:17, suggest this metaphor: "and the blood of Jesus Christ his Son cleanseth us from all sin." Hence Charles wrote:

> The worst of the foulest slaves of sin
>   May this salvation know
> Thro' faith in Jesus' blood made clean
>   And wash'd as white as snow;
> Heathens, whene'er to Him they turn,
>   He takes their sins away,
> Exalted with us who long have borne
>   The burden of the day.

In a similar fashion, the "blood of Christ" was merged with purchase metaphors to describe how Jesus' saving death "bought us with blood":

> Salvation to God,
>   Who bought us with blood,
>   Through Jesus' name
> Acceptance, and pardon, and heaven we claim.

The Lamb of God

The phrase "Lamb of God" has several important biblical connections, which made it a rich and prominent phrase in Charles Wesley's hymns. For example, the lamb figures prominently in the pivotal Old Testament institutions and holy days. The great prophets continued to view "the lamb" as an intercessory image, and this development reached its pinnacle in the Suffering Servant songs of Isaiah, where the Servant of the Lord is described as "being brought as a lamb to the slaughter" (Isa. 53:7). The exclamation of John the Baptist, "Behold the Lamb of God which taketh away the sins of the world" (John 1:29, 36), was formed in this same prophetic mold. The "taking away" aspect may have been drawn from the Levitical "scapegoat ceremony" in which the sins of the people were symbolically transferred to the head of a scapegoat, who "bears upon his head all their iniquities unto a land not inhabited" (Lev. 16:20-22). Charles Wesley saw this as an acted parable of Christ's substitutionary sin-bearing. Jesus Christ was viewed as "the Lamb who died for us," or who died for "the whole world." His death was viewed as a sacrifice, which Charles saw foreshadowed in the Levitical rites:

> The fiery law by Moses given,
>   Was thundered in a voice from heaven;
> In shadowy types and victims slain,
>   Which could purge our sinful stain,
> It only pointed at the Lamb;
>   But grace and truth by Jesus came.

Because of the sacrificial connection which Charles drew between the Levitical sacrifices and Good Friday, he often described Jesus as "a sin atoning Lamb," or "a lamb which blood atonement makes." Continuing the Levitical sacrifice imagery, Wesley described the Lamb of the New Covenant as being "without spot or blemish," who was "slaughtered" or "slain." In his hymns the "blood of the Lamb" was often said to be the agency of Christ's intercession, and hence that blood was described as an "oblation" which "ascertains our salvation." It was also "the ransom" which was paid to purchase our pardon. In a similar way the sacrificial death of "the Lamb" took away our sin and guilt:

> His offering did thy guilt remove,
>   The Lamb that on that altar lay,

A spark of Jesus' flaming love
 Hath purg'd thy world of sin away.

Charles employed the Pauline phrase in 1 Corinthians 5:7, where Christ is described as "our Passover . . . sacrificed for us":

Christ, our Passover, is slain,
 To set His people free,
Free from sin's Egyptian chain,
 And Pharaoh's tyranny;
Lord, that we may now depart,
 And truly serve our pardoning God,
Sprinkle every house and heart,
 With thine atoning blood.

Christ the Victor

While there are not an overabundance of biblical texts that view Christ's atonement as a victory by armed conflict over the forces of evil, darkness, and death, there is within the Pauline corpus some indication that these images played a role in the apostle's thinking.[1] Likewise, that corpus described the Christian life as fighting the good fight (1 Cor. 15:32), and being protected by the armor of God (Rom. 13:12; 2 Cor. 6:7; Eph. 6:11ff.) and armed with the sword of the Spirit (Eph. 6:17). These phrases and others which were seemingly unrelated provided Charles Wesley with a rich palette of terms with which to paint as he described Christ's atoning victory over sin and death. The Lamb of God is also the Lion of Judah, who wins a great victory over the forces of darkness and evil. In the following passage, for example, *Christus Victor* imagery merges with purchase language to describe the liberating effects of the atonement:

Can'st thou thy lost powers restore,
 Rise, go forth and sin no more?
Never, never can it be,

---

1. Galatians 1:4, Colossians 22:15, Romans 8:35ff., Philippians 2:10, and 1 Corinthians 15:24 offer some hints that the apostle regarded Jesus Christ's saving death as a victory over the "principalities and powers."

God alone can set thee free!
God alone the work hath done,
    Fought the fight, the battle won;
All thy sins on Him were laid,
    Happy soul, for guilt set free,
Jesus died for thee, for thee!
    Jesus does for thee atone,
Points thee to th'eternal crown,
    Speaks to thee the kingdom given,
Kingdom of an inward heaven,
    Glory, joy, unmerited peace,
All-victorious righteousness.

A crucial dimension of Christ's victory on the cross was the fact that it meant (and means) liberation from the tyranny of Satan and sin: "Satan's strongholds o'erthrown shall be, / The poor shall on their ruins tread, / Lead captive their captivity, / From all their sins forever freed." This liberating victory over Satan and sin was a triumph that could be realized within the believer as sanctification. And in Charles's hymns liberation themes merged with his constant concern for sanctification:

Son of God, Thine anger show
    Against our foes and thine,
Manifest here below,
    Fulfill thine own design.
Satan's reign and works to end
    Thine own almighty grace employ,
Thrust his out, this inbred fiend,
    And all our sins destroy.

An important corollary to this perspective of Jesus as Victor in a cosmic warfare was the corresponding emphasis upon the Christian's life as a struggle against the tyranny of evil, sin, and death. Hence, Christians are described as soldiers of Christ who are armed by Christ for victory in this life:

Soldiers of Christ, arise,
    And put your armour on,
Strong in the strength which God supplies

Through His eternal Son,
Strong in the Lord of Hosts,
    And in His mighty power,
Who in the strength of Jesus trusts
    Is more than conqueror.

Christ the Font of Our Salvation

Charles Wesley, like his elder brother, blended justification and sanctification themes together in his theology of redemption. In the case of the imagery Charles developed around Christ as the font or fountain of our salvation, he wove several scriptural allusions into a new and fresh application of what the Bible affirmed in passages like John 7:37, where Jesus is described as washing away our sin, and Revelation 21:6, where a fountain filled with the water of life is depicted. The imagery of the fountain filled with blood in Charles's hymns stressed the cleansing and life-giving power of Jesus' sacrificial blood. The source of this cleansing "purple tide" was, in Charles's hymns, the wounded side of Jesus Christ:

Weary souls, who wander wide
    From the central point of bliss,
Turn to Jesus crucified,
    Fly to those dear wounds of his,
Sink into the purple flood,
    And rise into the life of God.

These same images emerged as Charles linked the "purple tide" of Christ's cleansing and life-giving blood directly to Jesus' wounded side, and atonement:

Plunge me into the purple tide
    Of thy atoning blood;
Take me, Lord, into thy side,
    And bring me pure to God;
If thou hast not died in vain,
    The purchase of thy passion seize;
And bid me die in peace.

The description in the Gospel of John of the crucifixion of Jesus Christ and the piercing of his side (John 19:34), with the accompanying effusion of water and blood, prompted Charles to write, "A fountain deep and wide/T'was open'd by the soldier's spear,/In my Redeemer's side!" In this "blended stream" which flowed from the Savior's side, the believer was both justified and sanctified by faith:

> The stream that from Thy wounded side
>   In blended blood and water flow'd,
> Shall cleanse whom it first justified,
>   And FILL us with the life of God.[2]

Physician of Our Souls

Charles Wesley often described Jesus Christ as our "kind Physician," and used that medical imagery for explaining the saving effects of Jesus' death. The biblical foundation for this motif was rooted in a saying of Jesus: "They that are whole need not a physician" (Mark 2:17), meaning that Jesus came into the world as a physician comes to the sick. Wesley elaborated this imagery beyond the depiction of the biblical text by blending it with other biblical passages and allusions. In each case the singer or reader of Charles's poem is depicted as recognizing a "need" (in contradistinction to those mentioned in the original biblical passage). For example:

> I have need of a physician;
>   Jesus, my physician be:
> Help me in my lost condition,
>   Sin's severe extremity;
> Sick to death of pride and passion,
>   Desperate, Lord, to thee I cry;
> With thine uttermost salvation
>   Save, or I forever die.

Charles often merged the intercessory imagery of Christ as physician with those healing themes provided by the parable of the Good Samaritan. In

---

2. This blended effusion imagery, which is based in the biblical text, may also be an allusion to the Anglican practice of mingling water with the wine in the communion chalice.

this development Christ becomes the "Good Physician" who saves and heals the wounded traveler:

> Saviour of my soul, draw nigh,
>   In mercy haste to me;
> At the point of death I lie,
>   And cannot come to Thee,
> Now Thy kind relief afford,
>   The wine and oil of grace pour in;
> Good Physician, speak the word,
>   And heal my soul of sin.

This development also seems to have been quite prominent in Charles Wesley's preaching, but since none of his sermons on the Good Samaritan passage have survived we are forced to rely on his journal's description of him preaching this motif. In his journal entry for February 11, 1748, for example, Charles reported, "I showed them their case and their physician in the wounded traveler and the Good Samaritan." For Charles Wesley to locate this healing metaphor in the atonement of Christ meant that Jesus' blood was healing or "balmy blood":

> Nature's impatient condition
>   Feels my paralytic soul
> Find in Christ a kind Physician;
>   By the word of faith made whole,
> Joyful tidings of salvation
>   Come and speak my pardon sure,
> Faith in Jesus' blood passion,
>   Minister'd the perfect cure.

A second important pairing emerged in this same connection between the Physician and Good Samaritan imagery. The "oil and wine" the Samaritan used to succor the traveler's wounds (Luke 10:34) also became a standard Wesleyan idiom for the healing power of God's grace. For example, Charles wrote: "Now Thy kind relief afford,/The wine and oil of grace pour in;/Good Physician, speak the word,/And heal my soul of sin." This imagery was carried beyond the Luke text and was applied throughout the Wesleys' writings; often wherever sin was construed as sickness and salvation was considered healing, the "oil and wine" were applied.

Theology of the Cross

The Wesley brothers, like many Christians before them, placed great emphasis on the cross of Jesus Christ as a focal point in their theology. Not only was the cross God's decisive act in human history, whereby "God was in Christ reconciling the world to himself" (2 Cor. 5:19); the cross also marked out the conscious pattern of the Christian disciple's life. Building on the model of passages like Matthew 16:24, Mark 8:34, and Luke 9:23, Charles called upon the Christian to be "conform'd to an expiring God":

> Conform'd to an expiring God
>   We who feel his sprinkled blood
> The same distress abide:
>   And every soul that Jesus knows
> Partakes his bitterest pangs and woes
>   Together crucified.

For Charles, Christians not only embrace the pattern of Christ's selfless service and self-giving life, they also seek conformity to Christ in the character they develop as they bear unmerited suffering in this life. In this process of cross-bearing they "more and more like Jesus grow" in preparation for Christian Perfection:

> 3. While I thus my Pattern view,
>   I shall bleed and suffer too,
>   With the Man of Sorrows join'd
>   One become in heart and mind.

> 4. More and more like Jesus grow,
>   Till the Finisher I know,
>   Gain the final Victor's wreath,
>   Perfect love in perfect death.

For John and Charles Wesley, the atonement of Jesus Christ was a divine event in human history which was "received" by faith with transforming results. Through faith in the "blood of Christ" Christians are not only justified by God and reconciled to God, they embark on a process of sanctification whereby the whole of their inner and outer life gradually comes into conformity with that of Jesus Christ.

QUESTIONS FOR REFLECTION

1. What images or metaphors do you find helpful for understanding the atonement of Jesus Christ?
2. What do you think about the Wesleys' willingness to speak so frankly about "the blood of Christ"? What does that phrase mean to you?
3. How are we included in Christ's victory over sin and death?
4. What do Christian theologians mean by "a theology of the cross"?
5. In what sense do Christian disciples also have a cross to carry?

FURTHER READING

Maddox, Randy. *Responsible Grace* (Nashville: Abingdon/Kingswood, 1994), chapter 4: "Christ — An Atonement for Sin."

Rattenbury, John E. *The Evangelical Doctrines of Charles Wesley's Hymns* (London: Epworth Press, 1941), chapters 10-11.

CHAPTER TEN

One Glorious God in Persons Three

THE TRINITY

There are Three that bear record in heaven.

1 John 5:7

John and Charles Wesley lived, ministered, and wrote during an era when rationalism was becoming extremely influential in English intellectual culture and religion. The Enlightenment had come to England through the work of philosopher-theologians like John Locke (1632-1704). Now human reason and experience became, increasingly, the touchstone and basis for all knowledge. In religion this meant that mysterious matters like the doctrine of the Trinity became focal points for doubt and criticism. In some quarters of Anglican Christianity, supernaturalism was beginning to be replaced with naturalism, and classical Christianity began to evolve into Deism.

In its attempt to meet the challenges of rising rationalism, Christian orthodoxy, as Ronald Stromberg put it, "gambled on reason." Christians like Edward Cherbury (1583-1648) mounted rational defenses of Christian faith by pointing to natural evidences for it. But in this process the place that had been occupied by biblical revelation became imperiled, and human reason began to reign supreme. The version of Christianity that Cherbury advocated for actually sounded very much like a variety of Deism.[1]

As the Wesleys were studying at Oxford University works like John

---

1. It can be summarized by five main assertions: 1. There is a Supreme Power, whom we may call God. 2. This Sovereign Power must be worshipped. 3. Virtue combined with piety is the best part of Divine worship. 4. All human vices are hateful to God, and should be expiated by repentance. And 5. There are rewards and punishments beyond this earthly life.

Toland's *Deism: Christianity Not Mysterious or a Treatise Showing That There is Nothing in the Gospel Contrary Nor Above It, and That No Christian Doctrine Can Be Properly Called Mysterious* (1696) and Matthew Tindal's *Christianity As Old As Creation* (1732) became influential. Christianity was being reconfigured as a "natural religion" that coincided with the dictates of human reason, and was therefore not "miraculous" nor "mysterious." It was deemed "as old as creation" because it was thought that there was nothing genuine in the teachings of Jesus that went beyond the highest dictates of natural reason and the human conscience.

As the eighteenth century wore on, the impact of rationalism upon Christianity became increasingly more pronounced as important anti-trinitarian spokesmen like the Presbyterian Joseph Priestley (1733-1804) and the Anglican Theophilus Lindsey (1723-1808) emerged and gained a wide hearing. Priestley, who is probably now more famous as the scientist who discovered oxygen, was an influential Enlightenment thinker who published more than 150 works on various topics of philosophy, science, and religion. Priestley's friendship, support, and patronage of Lindsey and his Unitarian views led to the latter's establishing the first self-avowedly Unitarian congregation in London in 1774. The Wesleys' desire to be "Bible Christians" and exponents of "Scriptural Christianity" ran counter to these developments, and yet their theology was profoundly shaped by them.

While both John and Charles address the doctrine of the Holy Trinity in particular works — John in his standard sermon No. 55, "On the Trinity," and Charles in three separate collections of hymns — their real response to the anti-trinitarian impulses around them is to be found in the "truly Trinitarian balance" that is implicit in all their writings and in the very structure of their theology. Randy Maddox sees the Trinity imbedded in Wesleyan theology through "(1) reverence for the God of Holy Love and for God/Father's original design for human life, (2) gratitude for the unmerited Divine Initiative in Christ that frees us from the guilt and enslavement of our sin, and (3) responsiveness to the Presence of the Holy Spirit that empowers our recovery of the Divine Image in our lives." And Kenneth Collins reminds us that John Wesley was principally concerned with the revealed truths about the Trinity, which led to an emphasis (which he shared with Charles) on "the economic Trinity" — that is to say, the function that the Triune God plays in the process of human salvation — more than the "immanent Trinity," the more speculative aspects of the doctrine.

In 1742 the Wesleys published a "Hymn to the Trinity" in their *Hymns and Sacred Poems*. It voices a strong note of praise and thanksgiving for the Triune work of God in our salvation. Father ("God of unexhausted grace"), Son ("Suffering, sin-atoning God"), and Holy Spirit ("Holy Ghost, set to Thy seal") are each celebrated in a separate stanza of the hymn. The concluding verse brings all three Persons of the Trinity together for praise and celebration:

> 4. Father, Son and Holy Ghost,
>   Thy Godhead we adore,
>   Join with the triumphant host
>   Who praise Thee evermore;
>   Live, by heaven and earth adored,
>   Three in One, and One in Three,
>   Holy, holy, holy, Lord,
>   All glory be to Thee!

Here begins the Wesleyan tendency to affirm the saving work of the Triune God as revealed in Scripture, in order to celebrate and praise the Holy Trinity — but *not* to try to explain it.

This same tendency is seen in a small collection of occasional hymns entitled *Gloria Patri, and etc., Or Hymns to the Trinity,* which Charles published in 1746. In these twenty-four short hymns, once again the main emphases are upon the divinity and equality of the Three-in-One God who is to be praised rather than explained. For example, hymn No. 5:

> To God who reigns enthroned on high,
> To His dear Son who deign'd to die
>   Our guilt and misery to remove,
> To that blest Spirit who life imparts,
> Who rules in all believing hearts,
>   Be endless glory, praise, and love!

And again in hymn No. 23:

> 2.   The Three that are One
>   In a *manner unknown*
>   The Substance Divine in a mystery own,
>   Till in Him we remove
>   To His presence above,
>   And eternally plunge in the depths of His love.

The Wesleys' next offering in this vein was *Hymns on the Trinity,* published in 1767. This collection was occasioned in part by the publication of *The Catholic Doctrine of the Trinity proved by above a hundred short and clear arguments expressed in the terms of Holy Scripture, compared in a manner entirely new* (1754), which the Wesleys greatly admired. This theological tome provided the raw material and the biblical passages that formed the basis of the Wesleys' hymns. Following the book's outline, the Wesleyan hymns are arranged under the following headings: "The Divinity of Christ," "The Deity and Personality of the Holy Ghost," "Objections answered with arguments taken from the Divine Unity, Attributes and Will of God," and "Passages from Scripture which unite their beams in one common centre, the Unity of the Trinity, which unity is not metaphorical, and figurative, but strict and real." The outline of this hymnal communicates well its fundamental theological assertions: The Father, Son, and Holy Spirit are all one God, and are equally divine. They function as a plurality of three persons, within the unity of the Godhead. They are, to use a common Wesleyan phrase, "the Three-in-One God." John Wesley would subsequently use ten of these same hymns in his *Collection of Hymns for the Use of the People Called Methodists* (1780).

The first section, on "The Divinity of Christ," offers fifty-seven hymns based on a great variety of scriptural passages. Hymn No. 11 of this section, for example, is based on John 3:29 and Isaiah 54:5. In it Charles entered into conversation with doubters to affirm that Jesus the Son and Jehovah are indeed one and the same God:

1. Bridegroom of His church, and Head,
     And Husband is the Lord,
   By the universe He made
     Acknowledged and adored,
   The One God for ever bless'd,
   Supreme, omnipotent I AM,
   God made flesh and manifest
     On Earth in Jesus' name.

2. Different from the Father then
     Is Christ another God?
   No: Jehovah dwelt with men,
     And bought us with His blood:
   Christ the true Jehovah was,

And is, and shall be evermore:
God expiring on a cross
   Let earth and heaven adore.

The second section of *Hymns on the Trinity* offers thirty-three hymns on "The Divinity of the Holy Ghost." These hymns too are introduced by one or more passages from Scripture, which supply some of the raw material from which the hymn is developed. Hymn No. 53, which is based on John 14:20 ("At that day ye shall know that I am in My Father, and you in Me, and I in you,"), is a good example of the hymns that comprise this section. It stresses the divinity of the Holy Spirit in the context of the indwelling and transforming presence of God:

1. Whenever our day of Pentecost
   Is fully come, we surely know
The Father, Son, and Holy Ghost,
   Our God, is manifest below:
The Son doth in the Father dwell,
   The Father in His Son impart
His Spirit of joy unspeakable,
   And lives for ever in our hearts.

2. Our hearts are then convinced indeed
   That Christ is with the Father One;
The Spirit that doth from Both proceed,
   Attests the co-eternal Son;
The Spirit of truth and holiness
   Attests His own Divinity:
And then the orthodox confess
   One glorious God in persons three.

The third section of this same hymnal offers twenty-two longer hymns on "The Plurality and Trinity of Persons." The plural grammatical form which *Elohim* ("God") takes in the Hebrew Testament provides the basis for this plurality, which Charles found in Bible passages drawn from the Old Testament. Seizing upon the "us" of passages like Genesis 11:6, 7 ("And the LORD said, Let US go down and there confound their language"), Charles stressed the plurality and unity of the divine persons in the Holy Trinity. In verse two, contemporary critics of the Trinity (Arians) — who confuse the "scripture doctrine" with their own delusions — are compared to those prideful humans who built the Tower of Babel in order to make their own way to heaven:

1. Let US, saith the Lord, descend,
    Let US their designs confound,
   Bring them to a shameful end,
    Cast their castles to the ground;
   Rebels, who the Three in One
    Dare, with learned pride deny,
   By a *Babel* of their own
    Confident to reach the sky.

2. Be it so, Thou glorious God,
    Three in One, and One in Three,
   Able to abase the proud,
    Come with all Thy majesty;
   Men who *Arian* blasphemies
    Dare the *scripture doctrine* name,
   Let their dire delusion cease,
    Sink to hell from whence it came.

The fourth section of hymns *On The Trinity* contains twenty-six hymns that emphasize "The Trinity in Unity." These too are loosely based on particular passages of Scripture that Charles Wesley felt suggested the unity of the three divine persons within the Holy Trinity. This short hymn, No. 106, based on three Pauline passages, uses the image of "the mind of Christ" to stress that the entire Godhead was unified and of one mind when it came to saving "all mankind":

Who know the thing by God design'd
    To us the mind of Christ is known,
To us is known the Spirit's mind,
    One with the Father and the Son,
The counsel of the Trinity
    Infallibly reveal'd we have,
And witness that the heavenly three
    Are ready all mankind to save.

The last section of fifty-two "Hymns and Prayers to the Trinity" manifests a slightly different tone than those "on" the Trinity. The last section of hymns is more doxological in tone, more full of praise and thanksgiving to the Triune God, and generally the focus of this celebration revolves around the topic of our salvation. In No. 7 in the collection, each person of the Trinity is praised in turn for a distinctive role in our salvation:

1. All hail, mysterious Trinity!
     Every person of the three
     In my salvation meets:
    The Father draws me to the Son,
    Accepts for Jesus' sake alone,
     And all my sins forgives.

2. The Son His cleansing blood applies,
     Breaks my heart, and bids me rise
     A penitent forgiven:
    The Holy Ghost His witness bears,
    Numbers me with the royal heirs,
     And gives a taste of heaven.

3. The Father multiplies my peace,
     Jesus doth my faith increase,
     And teaches me to pray;
    The Spirit purifies my heart,
    And makes me, Saviour, as Thou art,
     And seals me to Thy day.

4. Thou, only thus I surely know
     God was manifest below,
     The God of pardoning grace,
    Whom saints in persons three admire,
    Whom I with all that heavenly choir
     World without end shall praise.

John Wesley's chief contribution to this body of literature, beyond organizing and editing the hymns — and perhaps composing a few of them — was his "standard sermon" No. 55, "On the Trinity." Albert Outler, in his introduction to this sermon in *John Wesley's Works,* rightly reminds us that the historical and theological context of this sermon is to be found in Wesley's desire to locate himself in a middle ground between the natural religion of Deism and contemporary Arians on the one hand, both of whom denied the doctrine of the Trinity, and a previous generation of Anglican rational apologetics on the other, which followed rationalism too far into trying to explain and prove the doctrine and in so doing wound up losing the battle with critics of the Trinity.

In this sermon, written and published in 1775, Wesley took a minimalist approach to the doctrine of the Trinity. While avoiding the phrase "fundamental" truths, he urged that there are some revealed truths which "have such a close connection with vital religion" that they cannot be safely jettisoned. He considered that affirmation of the doctrine of the Trinity from the biblical text (a corrupted text, as it turns out)[2] of 1 John 5:7: "There are three that bear record in heaven, the Father, the Word, and the Holy Ghost: and these three are one." Having argued for the importance of the biblical revelation about the Triune God, Wesley averred, "I do not mean that it is of importance to believe this or that *explication* of these words. I know not that any well-judging man would attempt to explain them at all." While he affirmed the content and explication of the Athanasian Creed on the Trinity, he would not insist that a person must agree with that creed in order to have eternal life:

> I am far from saying, he who does not assent to this "shall without doubt perish everlastingly." For the sake of that and another clause I for some time scrupled subscribing to that creed, till I considered, (1) that these sentences relate to *willful* and not involuntary unbelievers — to those who, having all the means of knowing the truth, nevertheless obstinately reject it; [and] (2) that they relate only to the *substance* of the doctrine there delivered, not the philosophical *illustrations* of it.

Wesley also indicated that he would not insist on a person using the words "Trinity" or "Person" in affirming this doctrine "because I do not find those terms in the Bible." Rather than insisting upon any particular terminology, or a particular explanation of the doctrine, John Wesley insisted simply upon the affirmation of the plain words of Scripture: "I would insist only on the direct words, unexplained, just as they lie in the text: 'There

---

2. Modern versions of this same passage emend it to read: "There are these three witnesses, the Spirit, the water, and the blood; and these three agree." Modern scholars have argued that some ancient manuscripts were altered to support the reading that this passage is given in the KJV.

are three that bear record in heaven, the Father, the Word, and the Holy Ghost: and these three are one.'"

"Is the text genuine?" Wesley asked. "Was it originally written by the Apostle or inserted in later ages?" While admitting that "Many have doubted of this," John followed the argument of John Albert Bengel (1687-1752) in support of the trinitarian rendition of the text as it was given in the Authorized (King James) Version.[3]

Wesley then addressed a second argument: "Whatever becomes of the text, we cannot believe what we cannot comprehend." His reply to this argument was characteristically direct: "Here is a twofold mistake. (1) We do not require you to believe any mystery in this whereas you suppose the contrary. But (2), you do already believe many things which you cannot comprehend." Wesley offered various examples drawn from natural science and biology: the existence of the soul, the nature of light, the existence of air, the planet earth, the function of the human body, and more. In these things, and many others, people believe "the fact" of the matter, even though they cannot comprehend "the manner" of it — that is to say, people believe in the fact of its existence and importance, even though they cannot completely comprehend or explain it. This is how John would have us think of the Trinity. He found scholarly support in the writings of Dr. Peter Browne (d. 1735), who "has proved at large that the Bible does not require you to believe any mystery at all. The Bible barely requires you to believe such *facts,* not the manner of them. Now the mystery does not lie in the *fact,* but altogether in the *manner.*" Here John gave two examples of "the fact" of the Trinity as being required by the biblical text, while "the manner" of it remains an incomprehensible mystery. "For instance, 'God said, Let there be light; and there was light.' I believe it: I believe the plain *fact;* that there is no mystery at all in this. The mystery lies in the *manner* of it. But of this I believe nothing at all; nor does God require it of me." Again: "'The Word was made flesh.' I believe this fact also. There is no mystery

---

3. Wesley cited three arguments in support of the antiquity of this text, from Bengel, which John found convincing: "(1) that though it is wanting in many copies yet it is found in more, abundantly more, and those copies of the greatest authority. (2) That it is cited by a whole train of ancient writers of the time of St. John to that of Constantine. This argument is conclusive, for they could not have cited it had it not then been in the sacred canon. (3) That we can easily account for its being after that time wanting in many copies when we remember that Constantine's successor was a zealous Arian, who used every means to promote his bad cause, to spread Arianism throughout the empire; in particular erasing this text out of as many copies as fell into his hands."

in it; but as to the *manner, how* he was made flesh, wherein the mystery lies, I know nothing about it; I believe nothing about it. It is no more the object of my faith than it is of my understanding."

Moving more directly to the topic at hand, John applied this distinction between the revealed "fact" of the Trinity and the "manner" of its existence to the doctrine of the Holy Trinity:

> "There are three that bear record in heaven . . . and these three are one."
> I believe this *fact* also (if I may use the expression) — that God is Three and One. But the *manner, how,* I do not comprehend; and I do not believe it. Now in this, in the *manner,* lies the mystery. And so it may; I have no concern with it. It is no object of my faith; I believe just so much as God has revealed and no more. But this, the *manner,* he has not revealed; therefore I believe nothing about it. But would it not be absurd in me to deny the fact because I do not understand the manner? That is, to reject *what God has revealed* because I do not comprehend *what he has not revealed?*

The doctrine of the Trinity, Wesley averred, "is far from being a point of indifference, is a truth of the last importance. It enters into the very heart of Christianity; it lies at the root of all vital religion." Without the Trinity people cannot honor, esteem, and worship Jesus Christ as they do God the Father; without this, Wesley thought, we have no vital form of Christianity. Without the doctrine of the Trinity there is no work of the Holy Spirit in the believer's life and heart — there is no witness of the Spirit that one belongs to God and has been accepted by God. So again John urged: "But the thing which I here particularly mean is this: the knowledge of the Three-in-One God is interwoven with all true Christian faith, with all vital religion." Hence, John concluded:

> I know not how anyone can be a Christian believer till "he hath" (as St. John speaks) "the witness in himself" [1 John 5:10]; till "the Spirit of God witnesses with his spirit that he is a child of God" [Rom. 8:16] — that is, in effect, till God the Holy Ghost witnesses that God the Father has accepted him through the merits of God the Son — and having this witness he honours the Son and the blessed Spirit "even as he honours the Father" [John 3:23].

QUESTIONS FOR REFLECTION

1. What role does the doctrine of the Trinity play in your own Christian life and thought?
2. The Wesleys considered the doctrine of the Trinity to be a crucial Christian doctrine. Do you? Why or why not?
3. What do you think about John Wesley's willingness to distinguish between the "fact" and the form of the doctrine?
4. Do you encounter modern Deists, who look upon Jesus as a great moral teacher but not as the Second Person of the Holy Trinity? What would the Wesleys have to say to this approach?

FOR FURTHER READING

Maddox, Randy. *Responsible Grace* (Nashville: Kingswood/Abingdon, 1994), pp. 136-41.

Oden, Thomas. *John Wesley's Teachings,* 3 vols. (Grand Rapids: Zondervan, 2012), volume 1, chapter 1, "God."

Rattenbury, John E. *The Evangelical Doctrines of Charles Wesley's Hymns* (London: Epworth, 1941), chapter 7: "The Holy Trinity."

CHAPTER ELEVEN

I in Thy Temple Wait

THE MEANS OF GRACE

The gospel of Christ knows of no religion, but social; no holiness
but social holiness.

Preface, *Hymns & Sacred Poems,* 1739

In the afterglow of their conversion experiences of May 1738, and while
their sporadic preaching ministry was burgeoning into the Wesleyan revival in 1739, John and Charles prepared and published a manifesto of their
newfound faith. Ironically, it was not a collection of sermons, or a system-
atic theology, or even a theological treatise. It was a collection of hymns!
The dissemination of the Wesleyan revival through the production and
publication of many, many hymns was a part of the Wesley brothers' stated
desire to speak *ad populum* ("to the people") and to "the bulk of humanity."
Even as clergy and Oxford-educated men, the Wesleys viewed themselves
as men of the people, and they intended their message for common people. In eighteenth-century England, popular songs were among the social
media of the day. The Wesleys' hymnody fit well with that phenomenon
and played a major role in it.

The preface of their 1739 *Hymns and Sacred Poems* was probably
penned by John, but the hymnal, like most of their more than fifty years
of ministry, was a joint project. It is likely that Charles produced most
of the hymns and that John's editorial pen made them suitable for congregational use and publication. But we also know that John wrote original hymns, and that Charles was capable of editing his own work. The
preface warns that some of the verses contained therein were written at
a time when the authors relied too much on the work of "the mystic di-

vines." They were convinced, now, that in placing so much weight upon their own striving for righteousness — as was encouraged by the spiritual writers they were studying — "we therein greatly erred." Describing the change that their discovery of justification by faith in Jesus Christ and salvation by grace made in the ordering of their understanding of salvation, they wrote: "in truth, we are no more justified for the sake of one than of the other. For neither our own inward nor outward righteousness is the ground of our justification. Holiness of heart, as well as holiness of life, is not the cause, but the effect of it." Reversing the order suggested by William Law and other "mystic divines," the Wesleys now stressed that the "sole cause of our acceptance with God . . . is the righteousness and the death of Christ, who fulfilled God's law, and died in our stead. And even the condition of it is not (as they suppose) our holiness either of heart or life; but our faith alone; faith contradistinguished from holiness as well as from good works."

The preface also attacks the quietism and solitary, individualistic approach advocated by some of those "mystic divines." "Directly opposite to this is the Gospel of Christ. Solitary religion is not to be found there. 'Holy solitaries' is a phrase no more consistent with the Gospel than holy adulterers. The Gospel of Christ knows of no religion, but social; no holiness, but social holiness."

"Social holiness" committed the Methodists to an interconnection of small groups as well as to a progressive posture on social problems like alcohol abuse and slavery. The stirring conclusion to their famous preface weaves the Wesleyan emphasis upon justification by faith and social holiness into one whole fabric:

> Ye feel that by grace ye are saved through faith; saved from sin, by Christ formed in your hearts, and from fear, by His Spirit bearing witness with your spirit, that ye are the sons of God. Ye are taught of God, not to forsake assembling of yourselves together, as the manner of some is; but to instruct, admonish, exhort, reprove, comfort, confirm, and every way build up one another. Ye have an unction from the Holy One, that teacheth you to renounce any other or higher perfection, than faith working by love, faith zealous of good works, faith as it hath opportunity doing good unto all men. As ye have therefore received Jesus Christ the Lord, so walk ye in Him: rooted and built up in Him, and established in the faith, and abounding therein more and more.

Wesleyan Small Groups

The heart and soul of the Methodist movement, apart from the Wesleyan gospel as mediated through sermons and hymns, was the class meeting. The class meeting was a weekly gathering of ten to twelve Methodists who lived in the same geographic area. They would come together for prayer, singing, pastoral care, and Christian fellowship, all under the direction of a "class leader." The class leader was a layperson who had been trained for this role by local lay pastors, or by one of the Wesleys themselves. Those people who were awakened by Wesleyan evangelism were encouraged to join a Methodist Society, and they did that through joining a class. The Society was the gathering of all the Methodist classes in a particular Anglican parish or town. The Society typically met several times a week for preaching, teaching, and fellowship, but much of the spiritual growth and pastoral care of the early Methodists occurred in their individual classes.

As early as December 1738, John Wesley had begun establishing "band societies" — as he called them at that point. Subsequently these would be called "classes," and the term "bands" would be reserved for gatherings of ten to twelve mature Christians, segregated by gender, who would come together to encourage each other in Christian holiness and perfection. The guidelines the Wesleys issued in December 1738 give us a good idea of what they hoped would occur in the class meetings: "The design of our meeting is, to obey that command of God, 'Confess your faults one to another, and pray one for another, that ye may be healed.'"

> To this end, we intend: 1.) To meet once a week, at the least. 2.) To come punctually at the hour appointed, without some extraordinary reason. 3.) To begin (those of us who are present) exactly at the hour, with singing or prayer. 4.) To speak each of us in order, freely and plainly, the true state of our souls, with the faults we have committed in thought, word, or deed, and the temptations we have felt, since our last meeting. 5.) To end every meeting with prayer, suited to the state of each person present. 6.) To desire some person among us; to speak his own state first, and then to ask the rest, in order, as many and as searching questions as may be, concerning their state, sins, and temptations.

The Wesleys also supplied the classes with a set of questions to be put to everyone before admission to the Methodist class meeting:

Some of the questions proposed to every one before he is admitted among us may be to this effect: — 1.) Have you the forgiveness of your sins? 2.) Have you peace with God, through our Lord Jesus Christ? 3.) Have you the witness of God's Spirit with your spirit, that you are a child of God? 4.) Is the love of God shed abroad in your heart? 5.) Has no sin, inward or outward, dominion over you? 6.) Do you desire to be told your faults? 7.) Do you desire to be told of all your faults, and that plain and home? 8.) Do you desire that every one of us should tell you, from time to time, whatsoever is in his heart concerning you? 9.) Consider! Do you desire we should tell you whatsoever we think, whatsoever we fear, whatsoever we hear, concerning you? 10.) Do you desire that, in doing this, we should come as close as possible, that we should cut to the quick, and search your heart to the bottom? 11.) Is it your desire and design to be on this, and all other occasions, entirely open, so as to speak everything that is in your heart without exception, without disguise, and without reserve?

John and Charles also stipulated that while "Any of the preceding questions may be asked as often as occasion offers; the four following [questions are to be asked] at every meeting: 1.) What known sins have you committed since our last meeting? 2.) What temptations have you met with? 3.) How were you delivered? 4.) What have you thought, said, or done, of which you doubt whether it be sin or not?"

The conditions for membership in the Methodist Society were equally clear:

There is one only condition previously required in those who desire admission into these societies: a desire "to flee from the wrath to come, to be saved from their sins": But, wherever this is really fixed in the soul, it will be shown by its fruits. It is therefore expected of all who continue therein, that they should continue to evidence their desire of salvation. Thus we say to those who unite with us:

You are supposed to have the faith that "overcometh the world." To you, therefore, it is not grievous:

I. Carefully to abstain from doing evil; in particular:

1.) Neither to buy nor sell anything at all on the Lord's day. 2.) To taste no spirituous liquor, no dram of any kind, unless prescribed by a Physician. 3.) To be at a word both in buying and selling. 4.) To pawn nothing, no, not to save life. 5.) Not to mention the fault of any behind his back, and to stop those short that do. 6.) To wear no needless ornaments, such as rings, earrings, necklaces, lace, ruffles. 7.) To use no needless self-indulgence, such as taking snuff or tobacco, unless prescribed by a Physician.

II. Zealously to maintain good works; in particular:

1.) To give alms of such things as you possess, and that to the uttermost of your power. 2.) To reprove all that sin in your sight, and that in love and meekness of wisdom. 3.) To be patterns of diligence and frugality, of self-denial, and taking up the cross daily.

III. Constantly to attend on all the ordinances of God; in particular:

1.) To be at church and at the Lord's table every week, and at every public meeting of the Bands. 2.) To attend the ministry of the word every morning, unless distance, business, or sickness prevent. 3.) To use private prayer every day; and family prayer, if you are the head of a family. 4.) To read the Scriptures, and meditate therein, at every vacant hour. And: 5.) To observe, as days of fasting or abstinence, all Fridays in the year.

These questions and guidelines evidence the interconnection between what we might call "personal piety" and "public piety." They are designed to provide spiritual examination and counsel for individual members, in the context of a group that was going to hold them accountable for their private piety and public morality. These questions reflect the movement's concern for what the Wesleys called "works of piety" and "works of mercy." "Works of piety" were the spiritual disciplines and practices which the individual carried out to improve his or her personal piety. In a similar way, "works of mercy" were those religious practices (such as humanitarian service, alms-giving, etc.) which a person carried out for the help and improvement of others.

The "rules" of the bands and classes made these small groups into a kind of Protestant monastic community, in which each individual was dedicated to living a holy life. It meant that the spirituality and small-group experiences of the earlier Oxford Holy Club had been transplanted into the fertile soil of the Wesleyan classes and bands. The members of these classes were examined by one of the Wesleys or their traveling preachers on a regular basis, and some members were expelled for "disorderly walking." Those members who remained in good standing with the group were issued a "class ticket" which testified to their Christian character and experience. Some of these small, paper tickets, signed by John or Charles Wesley, have survived down to our own day.

The Means of Grace

There were essentially five spiritual disciplines the early Methodists practiced within their societies, classes, and bands. The Wesleyan "Minutes of Conversation," sometimes called "The Large Minutes," described these as "the means of grace," because they were opportunities to meet God in a particularly powerful way, and any time a person meets God, she or he can receive God's grace. In his standard sermon No. 16, "The Means of Grace," John Wesley defined the term in this way: "By 'means of grace' I understand outward signs, words, or actions ordained of God and appointed for this end — to be the *ordinary* channels whereby he might convey to men preventing, justifying, or sanctifying grace." These means of grace came in two specific varieties: the "instituted" and "prudential" means. The "instituted means" are those which Wesley believed that the Bible explicitly demands Christians use; "the prudential means" are those ordinances and practices that, while not commanded by Scripture, are to be followed by the wise and prudent person.

The "means of grace" came into sharper focus in 1739-40 as a controversy erupted in the infant Methodist movement. The so-called Stillness Controversy pitted the Wesleyan Methodists against their friends and colleagues in the Moravian Church. It is called the Stillness Controversy because a quietist spirituality had taken root among the Moravians — causing many of them to eschew external Christian practices (like going to church, taking the sacrament, etc.) for fear of trusting in them and hence turning those practices into idols. Concerned about falling into works-righteousness, the "Stillness" people waited in stillness and inactivity before the Lord rather than meeting God in the established means of grace. The Wesley brothers voiced some sympathy for the "Stillness" concern, for not obsessing over Christian ordinances or turning to good works used to merit salvation. But their sympathy with Anglican spirituality ran too deep for the Wesleys to break off from using the means of grace. In fact, they eventually felt forced to break fellowship with "the Still brethren" for the spiritual well-being of the Wesleyan Methodists.

John answered the "Still brethren" in "The Means of Grace," which he wrote and preached in 1741. John's proclamation begins by acknowledging that "some began to mistake the *means* for the *end,* and place religion rather in doing those outward works [rather] than in a heart renewed after the image of God." For many years, until recent times, "the number of those who *abused* the ordinances of God was far greater than those who *despised* them." Wesley intended to steer a middle way between the two extremes of abusing the means of grace by trusting in them as the means of salvation or despising their use because of their potential harm. Wesley was absolutely clear that there is no saving power in the means of grace by themselves: "we allow farther that the use of all means whatever will never atone for one sin; that it is the blood of Christ alone whereby any sinner can be reconciled to God; there being no other propitiation for sins, no other fountain for sin and uncleanness." In this, Wesley agreed with the statement by the Moravian quietist John Molther: "Christ is the only means of grace," and added: "he is the only *meritorious cause* of it — it cannot be gainsaid by any who know the grace of God." And yet the question at hand remains:

> We know this salvation is the gift and the work of God. But how . . . may I attain thereto? If you say, "Believe, and thou shalt be saved," he answers, "True; but how shall I believe?" You reply, "Wait upon God." "Well, but how am I to wait? In the means of grace, or out of them? Am I to wait for the grace of God which bringeth salvation by using these means, or by laying them aside?"

When Wesley searched the Scriptures for a reply to this dilemma he found (as he already knew he would) that the Bible urged its readers to meet God in prayer, in Scripture reading, and in partaking of the Lord's Supper.

John then turned his attention to the objections of the quietists, who had "despised" the means of grace by leaving them off. "The first and chief [objection] of these is, 'You cannot use these means (as you call them) without *trusting* in them.'" Ever the "Bible Christian," Wesley retorted, "I pray, where is this written? I expect you should show me plain Scripture for your assertion; otherwise I dare not receive it, because I am not convinced that you are wiser than God." After turning aside the second objection — that one cannot use the means of grace without trusting in them as an end in themselves — John took up the third objection:

It has been vehemently objected, thirdly, that Christ is the only means of grace. I answer, this is mere playing upon words. Explain your term, and the objection vanishes away. When we say, "Prayer is a means of grace," we understand a channel through which the grace of God is conveyed. When you say "Christ is the means of grace," you understand the sole price and purchaser of it; or, that "no man cometh unto the Father, but through him." And who denies it? But this is utterly wide of the question.

Regarding those means of grace, John continued:

As to the *manner* of using them, whereon indeed it wholly depends whether they should convey any grace at all to the user, it behooves us, first, always to retain a lively sense that God is above all means. Have a care therefore of limiting the Almighty. He doth whatsoever and whensoever it pleaseth him. He can convey his grace, either in or out of any of the means which he hath appointed.

Wesley's second concern was equally pointed:

[B]efore you use any means let it be deeply impressed on your soul: There is no *power* in this. It is in itself a poor, dead, empty thing: separate from God, it is a dry leaf, a shadow. Neither is there any merit in my using this, nothing intrinsically pleasing to God, nothing whereby I deserve any favour at his hands. . . . Settle this in your heart, that the *opus operatum* [the mere ritual observance], the mere work done, profiteth nothing; that there is no *power* to save but in the Spirit of God, no *merit* but in the blood of Christ; that consequently even what God ordains conveys no grace to the soul if you trust not in him alone. On the other hand, he that does truly trust in him cannot fall short of the grace of God, even though he were cut off from every outward ordinance, though he were shut up in the centre of the earth.

Finally, then, he urged,

in using all means, seek God alone. In and through every outward thing look singly to the *power* of his Spirit and the *merits* of his Son. Beware you do not stick in the *work* itself; if you do, it is all lost labour. Nothing short of God can satisfy your soul. . . . Remember to also use all the means *as means;* as ordained, not for their own sake, but in order to the renewal of your soul in righteousness and true holiness. If therefore they actually tend to this, well; but if not, they are dung and dross.

In a lengthy hymn of twenty-nine verses, Charles Wesley voiced the same opinion as his brother John about the means of grace. Charles began by repenting of an earlier, pre-conversion time when he had made "an idol" of the means of grace: "But I of *means* have made my boast,/Of *means* an idol made;/The spirit in the letter lost,/The substance in the shade." But this "works-righteousness" no longer reflects the state of the singer's heart and mind. He now sees God's grace differently. But what should he do? Should he disown God's "written Rule" which points Christians to the means of grace? Verses seven through ten voice Charles's desire to follow God's word and use the "holy ordinance": "9. Wildly shall I from Thine turn back,/A better path to find;/Thy holy ordinance forsake,/And cast Thy words behind?/10. Forbid it, gracious Lord, that I/Should ever learn Thee so!/No — let *me* with Thy word comply,/If I Thy love would know."

In this hymn, as in John's sermon, Christ is the only means of grace, but God in Christ comes to us through the means or channels that God has appointed for our use. The Scriptures point us towards God in Jesus Christ through the use of the means of grace. Therefore we should use them:

11. Suffice for me, that Thou, my Lord,
    Hast bid me fast and pray:
    Thy will be done, Thy name adored;
    'Tis only mine t'obey.

12. Thou bid'st me search the Sacred Leaves,
    And taste the hallow'd Bread:
    The kind commands my soul receives,
    And longs on Thee to feed.

13. Still for Thy loving kindness, Lord,
    I in Thy temple wait;
    I look to find Thee in Thy word,
    Or at Thy table meet.

14. Here, *in Thine own appointed ways,*
    I wait to learn Thy will:

Silent I stand before Thy face,
  And hear Thee say, "Be Still."

15. "Be still — and know that I am God!"
    'Tis all I live to know;
    To feel the virtue of Thy blood,
    And spread its praise below.

16. I wait my vigour to renew,
    Thine image to retrieve,
    The veil of outward things pass through,
    And grasp in Thee to live.

And so, for Charles, the means of grace are a "veil" through which comes God's grace. The same hymn voices Charles's desire to no longer "trust in the means." Instead he uses the means as a vehicle through which his saving trust in Jesus Christ is made manifest: "I *trust* in means no more./I trust in Him who stands between/The Father's wrath and me:/JESU Thou great eternal Mean,/I look for all from Thee."

The Instituted Means of Grace

In his sermon on the means of grace, John Wesley delineated what he believed to be the "chief" means: "prayer, whether in secret or with the great congregation; searching the Scriptures (which implies reading, hearing, and meditating thereon) and receiving the Lord's Supper, eating bread and drinking wine in remembrance of him."

In 1743, in their "Large Minutes," John and Charles gave a fuller explanation of their understanding of the means of grace, this time dividing them between those which were "instituted" and those which were "prudential." The former corresponded roughly to the list from John's earlier sermon. These means of grace, he believed, were "ordained by God." By this Wesley meant that the Bible commands its readers to use these means of grace as a part of their Christian discipleship. Hence Jesus' statement "when you pray" (Matt. 6:6) assumes the force of a command. Jesus also urged his hearers to "search the Scriptures" (John 5:39). Referring to the Lord's Supper, Jesus said, "Do this in remembrance of me" (Luke 22:19, 1 Cor. 11:24) — this too assumed the force of a divine command for the

Wesleys. Jesus' words "when you fast" (Matt. 6:16) suggest that his disciples would be fasting. And the saying "do not neglect assembling together" (Heb. 10:25) sounds like a clear direction from God. Based on passages like these as well as the traditions of the ancient church, the Wesleys considered prayer, searching the Scriptures, the Lord's Supper, fasting, and Christian conference (or fellowship) to be instituted by God for the use of Christ's disciples. These five disciplines received fuller explication in the "Large Minutes." Those disciplines termed "prudential" were thought to be less obligatory, in that there was no direct scriptural injunction to do them, but they were considered wise or "prudent" practices, which the Christian disciple would want to embrace in order to live a life of faith and holiness.

First on the Wesleyan list of instituted means of grace, or spiritual disciplines: "Prayer; private, family, public; consisting of deprecation, petition, intercession, and thanksgiving." The Wesleys prayed using both formal prayers, as from the Anglican *Book of Common Prayer,* and extemporaneous prayers. In the "Large Minutes," they asked a series of pointed questions suggesting how they wanted Methodists to pray: "Do you use private prayer every morning and evening? If you can, at five in the evening; and the hour before or after morning preaching? Do you forecast daily, wherever you are, how to secure these hours? Do you avow it everywhere? Do you ask everywhere, 'Have you family prayer?' Do you retire [to pray] at five o'clock?"

In his "Sermon on the Mount, part VI," which was based on Matthew 6:1-15, John Wesley addressed the topic of prayer extensively. Following the biblical text, he urged his listeners to pray privately, and to pray with meaning, for length without meaning and "vain repetitions" are reproved in the Scriptures. John reminded his hearers that "the end of your praying is not to inform God, as though he knew not your wants already; but rather to inform yourselves, to fix the sense of those wants more deeply in your hearts, and the sense of your continual dependence on him who only is able to supply all your wants." Furthermore, "it is not so much to move God — who is always more ready to give than you to ask — as to move yourselves that you may be willing and ready to receive the good things he has prepared for you." This same sermon concludes with a spirited exposition of the Lord's Prayer, and a nine-verse hymn, entitled "The Lord's Prayer Paraphrased," which served the same purpose:

> 6. Father, 'tis thine each day to yield
>   Thy children's wants a fresh supply;

Thou cloth'st the lilies of the field,
    And hearest the young ravens cry.
On thee we cast our care; we live
    Through thee, who know'st our every need;
O feed us with thy grace, and give
    Our souls this day the living bread.

The second spiritual discipline stressed by the "Large Minutes" is "searching the Scriptures." Here the Wesleys divided their questions into three categories shaped around "reading," "meditating," and "hearing" the Scriptures:

Reading: constantly, some part every day; regularly, all the Bible in order; carefully, with the *Notes;* seriously with prayer before and after; fruitfully, immediately practicing what you learn there?

Meditating: at set times? By any rule?

Hearing: every morning? Carefully; with prayer before, at, after; immediately putting in practice? Have you a New Testament always about you?

The third spiritual discipline that was embraced by the early Methodists as an instituted means of grace was the Lord's Supper (which was so important that it will be treated separately in the next chapter). The "Large Minutes" asked: "Do you use this at every opportunity? With solemn prayer before; with earnest deliberate self-devotion?"

The fourth spiritual discipline on this list was fasting. Here the "Large Minutes" simply asked: "how do you fast every Friday?" John Wesley's standard sermon No. 27, "Upon our Lord's Sermon on the Mount, Discourse VII," extensively addressed the topic of fasting because "of all the means of grace there is scarce any concerning which men have run into greater extremes than that of which our Lord speaks in the above mentioned words [Matt. 6:16-18]; I mean religious fasting. How have some exalted this beyond all Scripture and reason! And others utterly disregarded it, as it were revenging themselves by undervaluing as much as the former had overvalued it." As was typical with him, Wesley sought to steer a middle way between overvaluing and undervaluing fasting. To fast, John reminds us, means "in one single sense, . . . not to eat, to abstain from food." He showed his hearers that there are "degrees or measures of fasting." "But the time of fasting more frequently mentioned in the Scripture is one day, from morning till evening. And this was the fast commonly observed among the ancient Christians." He also described "abstinence" as a sort of fasting "which may be used when we cannot fast entirely, by reason of sickness, or bodily weakness. This is the eating little; abstaining in part; the taking a smaller quantity of food than usual." Another kind of abstinence, "or the lowest kind of fasting . . . is the abstaining from pleasant food." He gave a dozen spiritual and biblical reasons as to why we should fast. "But above all," John wrote, "we have peculiar reason for being 'in fastings often,' namely the command of him [Christ] by whose name we are called [Christian]. He does not indeed in this place *expressly* enjoin either fasting, giving of alms, or prayer. But his directions how to fast, to give alms, and to pray, are of the same force with such injunctions." In addition to its benefits, and in addition to our Lord's implied command, there is "still further motive and encouragement to the performance of this duty; even the promise which our Lord has graciously annexed to the due discharge of it: 'Thy Father, which seeth in secret, shall reward thee openly.'"

The fifth spiritual discipline described by the Wesleys' "Large Minutes" is "Christian Conference." Again, this practice is enjoined upon the reader by a series of pointed questions: "Are you convinced how important and how difficult it is to 'order your conversation right?' Is it 'always in grace? Seasoned with salt? Meet to minister grace to the hearers?' Do not you converse too long at a time? Is not an hour commonly enough? Would it not be well always to have a determinate end in view; and to pray before and after it?" Christian conversation, such as that which took place in the early Methodist classes, bands, and societies, was to be seasoned with grace, and to have a particular spiritual end in view. The Wesleys' guidelines about time and focus were designed to keep these opportunities for spiritual fellowship on topic, and hence fruitful.

The Prudential Means of Grace

The "prudential" means of grace offered by the "Large Minutes" were also phrased in the form of searching questions. They seem to be relatively self-explanatory, and yet they are extremely important for understanding the shape and focus of early Methodist piety:

(1) Do you steadily watch against the world, the devil, yourselves, your besetting sin? (2) Do you deny yourself every useless pleasure of sense, imagination, honour? Are you temperate in all things? Instance in food: do you use only that kind and that degree which is best for your body and soul? Do you see the necessity of this? (3) Do you eat no-flesh suppers? No late suppers? (4) Do you eat no more at each meal than is necessary? Are you not heavy or drowsy after dinner? (5) Do you use only that kind and that degree of drink which is best for both your body and soul? (6) Do you drink water? Why not? Did you ever? Why did you leave it off? If not for health, when will you begin again? Today? (7) How often do you drink wine or ale? Every day? Do you want [need] it? (8) Wherein do you "take up your cross daily?" Do you cheerfully bear your cross (whatever is grievous to nature) as a gift of God and labour to profit thereby? (9) Do you endeavor to set God always before you; to see his eye continually fixed upon you? Never can you use these means but a blessing will ensue. And the more you use them, the more you will grow in grace.

These practices had as their goal the living of a God-centered, other-oriented, self-disciplined way of life. Practices of simplicity and self-denial were considered a part of the path to Christlikeness.

The Wesleys' emphasis on "social holiness" involved each of their followers in the membership of a network of accountability groups, where works of piety and works of mercy were practiced. Not only did these groups run against the grain of the growing individualism of western culture, they also provided members with an accountability structure that helped them live as Christian disciples. The five instituted "means of grace" were a particularly important part of this program for holy living because they allowed the participant to receive God's gracious help in the process of sanctification. Through prayer (private, corporate, and family prayer), searching the Scriptures, receiving the Lord's Supper, fasting, and Christian conference, the Methodists employed "methods" for spiritual formation and maturity. By embracing the prudential means of grace, they prepared their hearts, minds, and bodies for the work to which God had called them.

QUESTIONS FOR REFLECTION

1. Do you believe that spiritual disciplines are important for your growth in grace and spiritual maturity?
2. Why did the Wesleys describe spiritual disciplines as "means of grace"?
3. What was the role played by discipleship groups in early Methodism? Do you belong to a small group? Why or why not?
4. What spiritual disciplines do you practice? How regularly?
5. What do you think about "prudential means of grace"? Do you practice any?

FOR FURTHER READING

Collins, Kenneth J. *The Theology of John Wesley* (Nashville: Abingdon, 2007), chapter 7, "The Church and Means of Grace."

Watson, David Lowes. *The Early Methodist Class Meeting: Its Origins and Significance* (Eugene, Ore.: Wipf & Stock, 2002).

Wesley, John. Standard Sermon No. 16, "The Means of Grace."

CHAPTER TWELVE

A Soul-Transporting Feast

THE LORD'S SUPPER

[I]t is the duty of every Christian to receive the Lord's Supper as
often as he can.

John Wesley, Standard Sermon No. 110

Both John and Charles Wesley were born and raised in the Church of England, and nowhere was this more evident than in the Wesleyan preference
for and practice of the Lord's Supper. As we observed in the previous
chapter, the Wesleys esteemed the Lord's Supper as a "means of grace."
John defined the phrase "means of grace" as "outward signs, words, or
actions ordained of God and appointed for this end — to be the *ordinary*
channels whereby he might convey to men preventing, justifying, or sanctifying grace." This meant, in practical terms, that the Lord's Supper not
only shows or demonstrates God's grace to us through a reenactment of
the events of the Upper Room, but it actually bestows God's grace upon
us, if we partake of it in repentance and faith. For the Wesleys the Lord's
Supper was an opportunity for meeting God through faith in Jesus Christ.
Through participation in the Lord's Supper, a person could be changed.

The Wesleys believed that the Lord's Supper could increase our awareness of God's grace, and in this sense enhance our Christian discipleship.
As John wrote in his sermon "The Means of Grace," "all who desire an
increase of the grace of God are to wait for it in partaking of the Lord's
Supper." In his sermon "Working Out Our Own Salvation" John made a
similar point: "At every opportunity be a partaker of the Lord's Supper.
'Do this in remembrance of him' [Luke 22:19, 1 Cor. 11:24], and he will
meet you at his own table."

In his sermon "The Duty of Constant Communion," John stressed "that it is the duty of every Christian to receive the Lord's Supper as often as he can." Wesley practiced what he preached in this regard: John Bowmer, who made an intensive study of John Wesley's letters and journals, estimated that Wesley received the Lord's Supper on the average of once every four or five days. The same sermon, which John wrote during his Oxford years and published fifty-five years later, gives several reasons for his convictions about "constant Communion."

> The first reason why it is the duty of every Christian so to do is because it is a plain command of Christ. That this is his command appears from the words of the text, "Do this in remembrance of me": by which, as the Apostles were obliged to bless, break, and give the bread to all that joined with them in these holy things, so were all Christians obliged to receive those signs of Christ's body and blood.

The reason for doing this, as Wesley pointed out, was "because the benefits of doing it are so great to all that do it in obedience to him; namely, the forgiveness of our past sins, and the present strengthening and refreshing of our souls." John explained at length:

> The grace of God given herein confirms to us the pardon of our sins by enabling us to leave them. As our bodies are strengthened by bread and wine, so are our souls by these tokens of the body and blood of Christ. This is the food of our souls: this gives strength to perform our duty, and leads us on to perfection. If therefore we have any regard for the plain command of Christ, if we desire the pardon of our sins, if we wish for strength to believe, to love and obey God, then we should neglect no opportunity of receiving the Lord's Supper. . . . Whoever therefore does not receive, but goes from the holy table, when all things are prepared, either does not understand his duty or does not care for the dying command of his Saviour, the forgiveness of his sins, the strengthening of his soul, and the refreshing it with the hope of glory.

With these significant benefits in mind, it was inconceivable for the Wesleys that Christian disciples would not want to receive the Lord's Supper at every opportunity.

Initially, the Methodists only received the Lord's Supper at Anglican parish churches, because the Wesley brothers refused to administer the sacrament in their Methodist Society rooms and preaching houses. They felt that offering the sacrament in non-Anglican venues would signal a drift towards separation from the Church of England. So the early Methodists trooped to their Anglican parish churches for their sacraments and preaching, and then marched off afterwards to their Methodist Society rooms for more preaching and Christian fellowship. Over time, however, this distinction broke down, and gradually the Wesleys administered the Lord's Supper in Methodist venues.

A Converting and Confirming Ordinance

The Wesleys and the early Methodists maintained that the Lord's Supper was both a converting and a confirming ordinance. Not surprisingly this affirmation drew them into conflict with various segments of the Christian community. Among fellow Anglicans the Lord's Supper was esteemed as a confirming ordinance of the church, intended to enhance and strengthen a person's spiritual life. But the Wesleys' insistence that the Lord's Supper was also a converting ordinance smacked of novelty to some of their Anglican contemporaries, like the Rev. Mr. Church. Rev. Church wrote and published a critique of "The Rev. Mr. John Wesley's Last Journal," which was so thorough that John felt forced to publish a point-for-point rebuttal and reply to Church's criticisms. Church delineated the supposed theological and practical errors which he found in John's published journal; the third of these has to do with the Lord's Supper and the proper reception of it. He did not believe that the Lord's Supper was a converting ordinance. Wesley replied to Rev. Thomas Church's criticism by simply reiterating what he had already written in his journal:[1]

> Friday, June 27 [1740], I preached on, "Do this in remembrance of me." It has been diligently taught among us, that none but those who are converted, who "have received the Holy Ghost," who are believers in the full sense, ought to communicate. But experience shows the gross falsehood of that assertion, that the Lord's Supper is not a converting ordinance. Ye are witnesses: For many now present know, the very beginning of your conversion to God (perhaps in some the first deep conviction)

1. The Rev. Mr. Church was a prominent Anglican cleric who was Vicar of Battersea and Prebendary of St. Paul's.

was wrought in the Lord's Supper. Now, one single instance of this kind overthrows that whole assertion.

The falsehood of the other assertion appears both from Scripture precept and example. Our Lord commanded those very men who were then unconverted, who had not yet "received the Holy Ghost," who, in the fullest sense of the word, were not believers, to do this in remembrance of him. Here the precept is clear. And these he delivered the elements with his own hands.

We can see elements of Wesley's "quadrilateral" at work. Scripture and experience disprove Church's assertion that the sacrament should not be offered to unbelievers — that it is, indeed, both a converting and a confirming ordinance. John taught on the same topic at length the next day, and stressed that all those who were seeking forgiveness of sins and renewal of their hearts and lives were proper recipients of the Lord's Supper. The critical edition of John Wesley's published journal is even more pointed in its summary of John's letter to Rev. Mr. Church: "But in later times many have affirmed that the Lord's Supper is not a *converting,* but a *confirming* ordinance. . . . But experience shows the gross falsehood of that assertion that the Lord's Supper is not a *converting* ordinance."

John Wesley wrote one of his most salient summaries of his eucharistic theology in his journal entry for June 28, 1739:

I showed at large (1) that the Lord's Supper was ordained by God to be a *means of conveying* to men either *preventing* or *justifying,* or *sanctifying grace,* according to their several necessities; (2) that the persons for whom it was ordained are all those who know and feel that they *want* [lack] the *grace* of God, either to restrain them from sin, or to *show their sins forgiven,* or to *renew their souls* in the image of God; (3) that inasmuch as we come to his table, not to *give* him anything but to *receive* whatsoever he sees best for us, there is *no previous preparation* indispensably necessary, but a desire to receive whatsoever he pleases to give; and (4) that *no fitness* is required at the time of communicating but a sense of our state, or our utter sinfulness and helplessness; everyone who knows he is *fit for hell* being just *fit to come to Christ,* in this as well as all other ways of his appointment.

In this way, then, John Wesley insisted that Scripture and experience demonstrated that the Lord's Supper was and is a converting and confirming ordinance of the church. In a similar way, by stressing that the Eucharist is a converting ordinance, Wesley thought that anyone who is conscious of personal sins and willing to repent of them is "fit to come to Christ" through this holy ordinance.

Hymns on the Lord's Supper

In 1745, over against the backdrop of the "Stillness Controversy," John and Charles Wesley published what would become the most complete statement of their theology of the Lord's Supper, and once again it was a hymn book. *Hymns on the Lord's Supper* (HLS) included a condensed version of a eucharistic handbook authored by Dr. Daniel Brevint entitled *The Christian Sacrament and Sacrifice; by Way of Discussions, Meditations, and Prayer upon the Nature, Parts, and Blessings of the Holy Communion,* plus 155 hymns composed by the Wesleys themselves. The book was a bestseller in the Wesleys' lifetime, running through ten successive editions. An abridgement of Brevint's book, probably prepared by John, formed the preface to the HLS. Then, borrowing the chapter heads of Brevint's book, the Wesleys divided their collection of hymns into six sections, which spelled out the nature and focus of the Lord's Supper. Adapted from Brevint's earlier, Anglican work, these six section headings describe well the main emphases of a Wesleyan approach to the Lord's Supper:

1. As it is a memorial of the sufferings and death of Christ
2. As it is a sign and a means of grace
3. The sacrament as a pledge of heaven
4. As it implies a sacrifice
5. Concerning the sacrifice of our persons
6. After the sacrament

As It Is a Memorial of the Sufferings and Death of Christ

To say that the Lord's Supper is a "memorial" is to follow the words of Jesus Christ, who said, "do this in remembrance of me" (1 Cor. 11:24). In so doing, we focus our attention through the "sign" (the elements of bread and wine) to the thing signified: the reconciling death of Christ. In Wesleyan terms, however, this "memorial" means more than a mere calling to mind of Christ's death. Time and space are no barriers to this sacramental memorial. It crosses those dimensions of time and space that separate us from Calvary and sets Christ's death in the midst of the congregation. Quoting from Brevint, the preface to HLS reports:

> The Lord's Supper was chiefly ordained for a *Sacrament.* (1) To *represent* the sufferings of Christ which are *past,* whereof it is a memorial. (2) To convey the first-fruits of these sufferings, in the *present graces,* whereof it is a *means.* And (3) to assure us of glory to come, whereof it is an infallible *pledge.*

In the sacrament, Christ's death is dramatically displayed before us in a manner that demands from us both repentance and faith:

> Hearts of stone, relent, relent
> 	Break by Jesus' Cross subdued,
> See His body mangled, rent,
> 	Cover'd with a gore of blood!
> Sinful soul, what hast thou done?
> Murder'd God's eternal Son!
>
> Yes, our sins have done the deed,
> 	Drove the nails that fix Him here,
> Crown'd with thorns His sacred head,
> 	Pierced Him with a soldier's spear,
> Made His soul a sacrifice:
> For a sinful world He dies.
>
> Shall we let Him die in vain,
> 	Still to death pursue our God?
> Open tear His wounds again,
> 	Trample on His precious blood?
> No, with all our sins we part:
> Saviour, take my broken heart!

Hence this "memorial" is a "setting before my eyes" that bridges the distance between past and present by communicating, in the vibrant language of Christian experience, the costliness and the effectiveness of Christ's death, as the Holy Spirit applies the significance of this event to the believing heart:

O what a soul-transporting feast
    Doth this communion yield!
Remembering here Thy passion past,
    We with Thy love are fill'd.

Sure instrument of present grace
    Thy sacrament we find,
Yet higher blessings it displays,
    And raptures still behind.

It bears us now on eagle's wings,
    If Thou the power impart,
And Thee our glorious earnest brings
    Into our faithful heart.

O let us still the earnest feel,
    Th'unutterable peace,
This loving Spirit be the seal
    Of our eternal bliss!

Quite a bit of ink has been spilled to ascertain and to prove exactly how the Wesley brothers conceived of Christ's presence in the Lord's Supper through the elements of the bread and wine. The HLS voices an unwillingness to breach the mystery of Christ's presence by offering a precise definition; instead it points to the effective results of Christ's presence in the Lord's Supper:

2. How He did these creatures raise,
    And make this bread and wine
  Organs to convey His grace
    To this poor soul of mine,
  I cannot the way descry,
    Need not know the mystery;
  Only this I know — that I
    Was blind, but now I see.

3. Now mine eyes are open'd wide,
    To see His pardoning love,
  Here I view the God that died

My ruin to remove;
Clay upon mine eyes He laid,
  (I at once, my sight received)
Bless'd and bid me eat the bread,
  And lo! My soul believed.

The Wesleys attacked the idea that Christ is physically present in the Communion elements. But Charles — the presumed hymn writer — would not say that Christ was absent from the Communion table, since Jesus himself set forth these "means" as vehicles of his life-giving love:

O God, Thy word we claim,
  Thou here record'st Thy name;
Visit us in pardoning grace,
  Christ, the Crucified, appear,
Come in Thy appointed ways,
  Come, and meet, and bless us here.

No local Deity
  We worship, Lord, in Thee:
Free Thy grace and unconfined,
  Yet it here doth freest move;
In the means Thy love enjoin'd
  Look we for Thy richest love.

Thus, for the Wesleys the Lord's Supper is Jesus Christ's "choicest instrument" through which he "doth all His blessings give." To describe how Christ's healing, life-giving presence is communicated through the Lord's Supper, the HLS turns to the account of Jesus healing a woman with a hemorrhage, through the instrument of her touching his own garment (Matt. 9:18-26):

Sinner, with awe draw near,
  And find thy Saviour here,
In His ordinances still,
  Touch His sacramental clothes;
Present in His power to heal,
  Virtue from His body flows.

Christ is present in the sacrament of the altar not because of his physical location in or around the elements, but by the power of the Holy Spirit, whose task it is to bear witness to Christ and to bring him to our remembrance (John 15:26):

> Come, Holy Ghost, Thine influence shed,
>   And realize the sign;
> Thy life infuse into the bread,
>   Thy power into the wine.
>
> Effectual let the tokens prove,
>   And made, by heavenly art,
> Fit channels to convey Thy love
>   To fill every faithful heart.

Just as outward eating fills and refreshes the inner person, so also "eating through faith" brings "the fullness of Christ" into the life of the Christian through the Lord's Supper.

As It Is a Sign and a Means of Grace

The Wesleys believed that the sacrament was a window through which God's grace shone into human hearts and lives. Standing on the foundation of Scripture and church tradition, John saw "the whole body of Christians being agreed that Christ had ordained certain outward means for conveying his grace to the souls of men." The Wesleys followed St. Augustine and the Anglican *Articles of Religion* in defining a sacrament as "an outward sign of an inward grace, and a means whereby we receive the same."

The "outward sign" refers to the Communion elements of bread and wine, which serve as "channels" or "instruments" which funnel "an inward grace" into the life of the church. This "inward grace" is nothing less than "all the benefits of Christ," which John Wesley typically described as "preventing, justifying, or sanctifying grace."

To identify "preventing grace" in the sacrament is to say that it has the power to convict and lead people to faith in Jesus Christ. To say that "justifying grace" is communicated through the Lord's Supper is to say that it can be a channel of God's saving and reconciling power. And to view Communion as an instrument of "sanctifying grace" is to indicate that it is one of the ways through which God leads his people "on to perfection" by purging their sin and sinful attitudes, and growing God's love and character within them.

In a similar way, the preface to HLS described the brothers' understanding of the sacrament by using three important verbs: "represent," "convey," and "assure." The sacrament functioned to (1) "represent the sufferings of Christ which are past," (2) "to convey the first fruits of these sufferings, in the present graces, whereof it is a means," and (3) "to assure us of glory to come, whereof it is an infallible pledge."

As we saw earlier, John's Standard Sermon No. 16, "On the Means of Grace," made it clear that the Wesleys wanted to steer a middle course between the extremes of those who "abused" the Lord's Supper by making it into an idol and a form of works-righteousness, and those who "despised" the sacrament through neglecting to use it as often as they had opportunity. For the Wesleys the sacrament was esteemed as "a sign and means of grace," and hence it was viewed as both a symbol and an instrument of God's redemptive power. For the Wesleys the Lord's Supper both "shows" and "bestows" the grace of our Lord:

> Author of our salvation, Thee
> > With lowly thankful hearts we praise,
> Author of this great mystery,
> > Figure and means of saving grace.
>
> The sacred, true, effectual sign,
> > Thy body and Thy blood it shows;
> The glorious instrument Divine
> > Thy mercy and Thy strength bestows.
>
> We see the blood that seals our peace,
> > Thy pardoning mercy we receive:
> The bread doth visibly express
> > The strength through which our spirits live.

The Sacrament as a Pledge of Heaven

For the Wesley brothers, calling the Lord's Supper "a pledge of heaven" was intended to focus our attention upon the restorative power of God's grace. The fellowship with Christ and Christians that we enjoy in the sacramental meal is like an appetizer of heaven — a little piece of heaven is broken off, shaped into a tangible promise of life with God, and placed in our midst. Or as Wesley wrote in hymn 97 in HLS: "We feel the earnest in our hearts!/Of our eternal rest." So those who enjoy God's salvation by grace alone participate in a bit of heaven on earth:

> Happy the souls to Jesus join'd,
>   And saved by grace alone;
> Walking in all Thy ways we find
>   Our heaven on earth begun.
>
> The church triumphant in Thy love,
>   Their mighty joys we know;
> They sing the Lamb in hymns above,
>   And we in hymns below.

The Eucharistic fellowship at the Lord's Table is a foretaste of the joy and glory which we will one day taste in full when "this perishable will have put on the imperishable, and this mortal will have put on immortality" (1 Cor. 15:51ff.). This foretaste of heavenly glory and God's kingdom among us prompts the poet to ask and reply: "Where shall this memorial end?/Thither let our souls ascend,/Live on earth to heaven restored,/Wait the coming of our Lord." Or as one of the Wesleys wrote:

> The light of life eternal darts
>   Into our souls a dazzling ray,
> A drop of heaven o'erflows our hearts,
>   And deluges the house of clay.

It is as though the Lord's Supper is a moment when the windows of heaven are thrown open wide and we are able to look in, full of anticipation.

As It Implies a Sacrifice

The Lord's Supper sets the death of Jesus Christ in a sacrificial context. It uses sacrificial language drawn from the Hebrew Scriptures to make theological sense of Jesus' saving death. The very words of institution, drawn from the Gospel narratives, make this point: "this is my body broken for you," and "this is my blood of the new covenant which is poured out for many for forgiveness of sins" (Matt. 26:26ff.).

Since Jesus identified the sacramental meal as an emblem of his own death, John Wesley's poetic imagination transposed the Cross of Calvary upon the church's altar:

The cross on Calvary He bore,
He suffered once to die no more,
    But left a sacred pledge behind:
See here! — It on Thy altar lies,
Memorial of the sacrifice
    He offer'd once for all mankind.

Father, the grand oblation see,
The death as present now with Thee
    As when He gasp'd on earth — Forgive,
Answer, and show the curse removed,
Accept us in the Well-beloved,
    And bid Thy world of rebels live.

But it is also clear in Wesleyan theology that this Eucharistic "grand obla-tion" is an emblem of Jesus' original once-for-all sacrifice and atonement, not a sacramental re-sacrificing of Christ on the altar of the church.

To stress that Jesus' death is "a sacrifice" is to draw attention to his role as redeemer, and to recognize that Jesus' death was a death he died for the forgiveness (atonement) of sins — a death he died not for himself, but for all of us:

All hail, Redeemer of mankind!
Thy life on Calvary resign'd
    Did fully once for all atone;
Thy blood hath paid our utmost price,
Thine all-sufficient sacrifice
    Remains eternally alone:

Angels and men might strive in vain,
They could not add the smallest grain
    To augment Thy death's atoning power,
The sacrifice is all complete,
The death Thou never canst repeat,
    Once offer'd up to die no more.

Concerning the Sacrifice of Our Persons

Just as the Lord's Supper points to and reminds us of Jesus Christ's giving of himself on our behalf, so also does a Wesleyan approach to the sacrament demand that we understand it as an act through which Christians give themselves to Christ. This act of utter self-consecration results in an inner renewal that touches every facet of a person's life:

> Take my soul and body's powers,
>   Take my memory, mind, and will,
> All my goods, and all my hours,
>   All I know, and all I feel,
> All I think, and speak, and do;
> Take my heart — but make it new.
>
> Now, O God, Thine own I am.
>   Now I give Thee back Thy own,
> Freedom, friends, and health, and fame
>   Consecrate to Thee alone. . . .

After the Sacrament

The Wesleys' eucharistic manual, *Hymns on the Lord's Supper,* closed with seven hymns designed to remind believers that even as we leave the Lord's Table, we do not leave God's presence. These hymns are full of the joy and adoration that flow into the Christian's life after having communed with Christ through his feast. These hymns dismiss us from the Lord's Table invigorated with the power for Christian living:

> 7. O, let Thy wondrous mercy's praise
>   Inspire and consecrate my lays [plans],
>   And take up all my lines and life;
>   Thy praise my every breath employ:
>   Be all my business, all my joy
>   To strive in this, and love the strife!

Real Presence

It is evident from their hymns and sermons that the Wesleys taught that the "real presence" of Christ was available to Christians in the Lord's Supper. This was and is a vital, life-giving, and transforming presence. They were not concerned to explain or define Christ's presence in the elements of Communion. This they viewed as a mystery, an event of the Holy Spirit. But they were clear that it was not a physical presence, based in the transformation of the elements into something other than bread and wine. As we saw in the hymns above, the Communion elements were esteemed as "a true and effectual sign" but "no local Deity." John was even more pointed in his rejection of the change of the elements (transubstantiation) in his polemical writings about Roman Catholicism. In his "Popery Calmly Considered," for example, John argued that "Scripture and [Christian] antiquity, then, are flatly against transubstantiation. And so are our very senses."

The Wesleys left their spiritual descendants a rich sacramental heritage. The brothers' fervor for the Lord's Supper was not based on sheer Anglican formalism, nor was it born in a threadbare sense of religious tradition. Rather, they embraced frequent Communion because it both "shows" (as a sign) and "bestows" (as a means) God's grace. The Lord's Supper communicates to us the benefits of Christ's death and resurrection, and demands that we respond to Christ in faith and commitment of our entire selves. The Wesleys enumerated these benefits as "preventing" (convicting), "justifying" (converting), and "sanctifying" (confirming and transforming) grace. Because of this powerful connection between Communion and the grace of God, the Wesleys insisted that frequent ("constant") Communion was a duty and blessed responsibility of all Christians.

QUESTIONS FOR FURTHER REVIEW

1. How do you think of the Lord's Supper? Do you agree with the Wesleys that it is "an effectual sign" which both shows and bestows God's grace?
2. Do you think of the Lord's Supper as a "means of grace"? Why? Why not?
3. How frequently do you participate in Communion? Why?

FOR FURTHER READING

Borgen, Ole. *John Wesley on the Sacraments* (Nashville: Abingdon, 1972), chapter 7.

Bowmer, John. *The Sacrament of the Lord's Supper in Early Methodism* (London: Dacre Press, 1951).

Rattenbury, John E. *The Eucharistic Hymns of John and Charles Wesley* (London: Epworth Press, 1948).

Wesley, John. Standard Sermon No. 110, "On the Duty of Constant Communion."

Wesley, John. Standard Sermon No. 16, "The Means of Grace."

CHAPTER THIRTEEN

Our Loving Labor

....

LIFE IN THE WORLD

I look upon all the world as my parish; thus far I mean, that in
whatever part of it I am, I judge it meet, right, and my bounden
duty, to declare unto all that are willing to hear the glad tidings
of salvation.

John Wesley, Letter, June 11, 1739

In the autumn of 1739, during the early stages of the Wesleyan revival, John
Wesley had three very tense interviews with the Anglican bishop of Bristol, Dr. Joseph Butler (1692-1752). Bishop Butler was a famous theologian
and conscientious defender of the Church of England. These interviews
were so sensitive and so embarrassing that Wesley excluded them from
his published journal. Initially, they survived only in the record of John's
early biographer, Henry Moore (1826), but in 1980 Frank Baker discovered
a manuscript copy (in John Wesley's handwriting) which gave some of
the details of these discussions. In both the published and unpublished
records Wesley was "called on the carpet" for his preaching justification by
faith and the new birth and for preaching in the parishes of other Anglican
clergy without their permission. The former charge was easily dismissed
when John Wesley explained his gospel, but the latter was not. The bishop
of Bristol put it bluntly: "You have no business here. You are not commis-
sioned to preach in this diocese. Therefore, I advise you to go hence." To
this warning, John Wesley replied: "My Lord, my business on earth is to
do what good I can. Wherever therefore I think I can do most good, there
I must stay so long as I think so. At present, I think I can do most good
here. Therefore, here I stay." Wesley continued: "As to my preaching here,

a dispensation of the gospel is committed to me, and woe is me if I preach not the gospel, wheresoever I am, in the habitable world. Your lordship knows, being ordained a priest, by the commission then received I am a priest of the church universal. And being ordained as Fellow of a College, I was not limited to any particular cure, but have an indeterminate commission to preach the Word of God to any part of the Church of England."

Refusing to have the scope of his ministry limited by Anglican parish boundaries, John Wesley developed his "world parish" concept. This broad understanding of pastoral responsibility was crucial to the Methodist itinerant ministry, and had been fomenting in John's thinking for several months. As Wesley had written in an earlier letter (to an unnamed recipient): "I look upon all the world as my parish; thus far I mean, that in whatever part of it I am, I judge it meet, right, and my bounden duty, to declare unto all that are willing to hear the glad tidings of salvation." And as John candidly told Bishop Butler that day: "I do not therefore conceive that in preaching here [in Bristol] by this commission I break any human law. When I am convinced I do, then it will be time to ask, 'Shall I obey God or man?'"

"I look upon the world as my parish" also speaks of a worldly Christianity, which emphasizes an approach to Christianity that seeks to make a real difference in the lives of people who live in the real world. To use a popular expression, this is not merely to go about trying to "save souls," as though people's bodies did not matter. Thus, early Methodist principles committed their adherents to the performance of "works of piety" (spiritual disciplines) as well as "works of mercy" (humanitarian service). For example, the "General Rules" committed the early Methodists to "doing good, by being, in every kind, merciful after their power; as they have opportunity, doing good of every possible sort, and as is possible, to all men; — to their bodies, of the ability which God giveth, by giving food to the hungry, by clothing the naked, by visiting or helping them that are sick, or in prison; — to their souls, by instructing, reproving, or exhorting all."

The Good Steward

In his sermon No. 51, "The Good Steward," John Wesley described all humans as debtors before God, our Creator. But our indebtedness is of a very special kind: we are to be good stewards (Luke 16:2) of all that God has bestowed upon us. Hence, "We are not at liberty to use what he has lodged in our hands as *we* please, but as he pleases, who alone is the Possessor of heaven and earth, and the Lord of every creature. We have no right to dispose of anything we have but according to his will, seeing we are not proprietors of any of these things. . . . [H]e entrusts us with them on this express condition, that we use them only as our Master's goods, and according to the particular directions which he has given us in his Word." It is on this basis that God has entrusted us with "our souls, our bodies, our goods, and whatever talents we have received. . . ." This is an important lesson, from which John expected his hearers to learn — as he had learned — that there was no "employment of our time, no action or conversation, that is purely *indifferent.* All is good or bad, because all our time, as everything we have, is *not our own.* All these are, as our Lord speaks, *ta allstria* [Greek], the property of another — of God, our Creator. Now these either are or are not employed according to his will. If they are so employed, all is good; if they are not, all is evil."

Both Wesley brothers became particularly serious about their Christian stewardship during their years in the Oxford Holy Club. John began to keep careful track in his diary of his time — down to the quarter hour — throughout his waking hours. And John habitually wore his hair long, parted in the middle, and without the convenience of a powdered wig — which was the mark of a gentleman (Charles wore a powdered wig). He and Charles both ate sparingly and of the most modest sort of food, in order to save money to give to the poor. While a fellow at Lincoln College, Oxford, John Wesley had the income of 30 pounds. Through frugality and careful living he found that he could live on 28 pounds, which allowed him to give away 2 pounds that year. The next year, Wesley's income doubled, but he found that through careful stewardship he could still live on 28 pounds, and so he gave 32 pounds to the poor. The third year John's income rose to 90 pounds, so keeping 28 pounds for his own living expenses meant he could give away 62. In the fourth year, John's income amounted to 120 pounds, but he once again kept his own expenses to that same 28 pounds, so that he was able to give 92 pounds away.

This same pattern continued when the brothers Wesley embarked upon their professional ministry. Both brothers continued to dress and eat modestly, rarely eating meat, so that they could conserve funds to be used for the relief of the poor. In 1771, when John Wesley published his first edition of his *Collected Works,* in 32 volumes, he earned 1400 pounds, but he still managed to live on 30 pounds and give all the rest of that money away. In 1776 John Wesley's income came under investigation by the British tax examiners; they could not believe that despite his extensive income, John owned no expensive silver plate (which they wanted to tax). In response to their enquiries, Wesley tersely wrote back, informing the government that he owned two silver spoons in London, and two more in Newcastle, and that was the full extent of his silver plate. They were astounded that someone who generated the income that John Wesley did could live so modestly.

When Charles married, in 1749, his future mother-in-law was so concerned about his Spartan lifestyle that she stipulated that Wesley had to be able to guarantee the availability of at least 100 pounds per year, so that her daughter could live in reasonable comfort. As Charles and Sally began raising children, they gradually adopted more of a middle-class lifestyle, so that their children could have some of the finer things of life — like proper clothes and expensive music lessons. Charles's rising expenses and John's continued frugality was the source of some friendly friction between the brothers.

John's pattern of frugal stewardship and liberal giving continued throughout his life; even in his old age, when the sales of the Wesleys' publications were making them a handsome income, John still gave almost all of the money away. Luke Tyerman, one of John's most careful biographers, estimated that over the course of his ministry Wesley gave away in excess of 32,000 pounds — which in today's money is equivalent to something like 1.5 million dollars. Answering criticisms that he was squirreling away funds for his own use, in 1743 John wrote, "if I leave behind me ten pounds (above my debts and the little arrears of my fellowship) you and all mankind [may] bear witness against me that 'I lived and died a thief and a robber.'" John was so sensitive to this criticism of laying up treasures on earth that when he thought he was on death's door, in November 1753, he penned this epitaph for himself: "Here lieth/The body of John Wesley/A Brand plucked out of the burning/Who died of a Consumption in the Fifty-first Year of his Age/Not leaving, after his Debts are paid, Ten Pounds behind him/Praying God be merciful to me, an unprofitable servant!" When John eventually did die, in 1791, he left almost no cash — after final expenses — and only a small amount of personal items that could be turned into cash. Tyerman put it this way: "Where were his hoardings, his money put out to interest, his landed household, and chapel property? He had none. He died, as he had lived, without a purse. He had been his own executor as far as possible; and now had nothing to bequeath, except what, in his lifetime, could not easily be turned into current coin."

Social Sin

John Wesley looked to the human will for the root of sin and misery in society (in contradistinction to societal or contextual causes). He responded to the question, "Why is there *pain* in the world?" by pointing directly to human sin. In a similar way, "the origin of evil" could be traced to the Edenic Fall, which "God permitted in order to a fuller manifestation of his wisdom, justice, and mercy, by bestowing upon all who would receive it an infinitely greater happiness than they could possibly have attained, if Adam had not fallen." But Wesley's emphasis upon the personal basis of sin was not so pervasive that he was blind to systemic injustice and societal evil.

John's collected sermons offer to us important test cases for looking at his approach to human sin in the collective or societal sense. The first issue is easily identified by the title of one of his later sermons, "National Sins and Miseries" (No. 111). It traces the impact of human sin beyond the individual into society at large. In Wesley's view, the "mystery of iniquity" has corrupted all facets of human history, including the church. His sermon on "The Reformation of Manners" (No. 352), which was delivered before a reformatory society by that same name, offered a direct — and admittedly simplistic — solution to the problem: "So far as . . . righteousness in any branch is promoted, so far is the national interest advanced. So far as sin, especially open sin, is restrained, the curse and reproach are removed from us."

Wesley's approach to the evil in human society began with the Word of God and personal piety, and it also extended beyond what others considered his appropriate field of influence to his urging legislation for the promotion of righteousness and restraint of evil. Perhaps in our own day we will not feel the full force of the scandal Wesley felt in matters like "buying and selling on the Lord's Day." Perhaps issues like global hunger or apartheid move us more acutely. But a clear pattern emerges in these sermons of a deep awareness of the way in which the selfish attitudes or immoral actions of a few can abridge the justice and threaten the well-being of the many.

John Wesley was also willing to see some of the faults of British colonialism: "We have carried our laurels into Africa, into Asia, into the burning and frozen climes of America. And what have we brought thence? All the elegance of vice which neither the eastern or western world could afford."

Women's Roles

Social restrictions upon women were quite severe at this time. Women were barred from higher education and hence from most professions and from most public roles. As in the Victorian Era that followed, women's roles were most often relegated to the domestic sphere. Because religion was seen as a part of the domestic life of the Christian family, the eighteenth century did grant women religious roles associated with the home and family. Women, for example, could and did teach their children to pray, to read the Bible, and to attend church; both John and Charles were taught to read the Bible and pray by their mother, and they wrote to her — instead of their learned father — when they had questions about their spiritual life. Doctrinal matters were directed to their father, Samuel, but practical questions about Christian living were directed to their mother, Susanna.

In the absence of their husbands, eighteenth-century English wives could and did lead family devotions. Both John and Charles saw an example of this development in 1711. When their father was away in London attending Convocation, their mother started reading to the family (which included the servants) from the Bible and from spiritual authors. The servants told their families about this development, and they asked permission to attend; some were spiritually awakened in this process. They told others about Mrs. Wesley's unauthorized meetings, and they too asked permission to attend. Within a few weeks nearly a hundred people were attending evening prayers led by Susanna Wesley. When Mr. Inman, the ineffective curate that Samuel Wesley had hired to replace him in his absence, got wind of these events, he wrote to Samuel in London, complaining that his wife was holding public meetings. Samuel wrote an immediate directive to Susanna telling her to stop what she was doing because it was being construed as a public meeting. He suggested that she allow a male parishioner to read and lead in her place. This suggestion clearly irritated her, and she wrote a spirited, point-by-point reply to Samuel's missive.

Samuel's objections to her Sunday evening meetings were, as she described them, three: "first, that it will look particular; secondly, my sex; and lastly, your being at present in a public station and character." Her reply to her husband's second point is particularly instructive: "To your second, I reply that as I am a woman, so I am also mistress of a large family. And though the superior charge of the souls contained in it lies upon you as head of the family and their minister, yet in your absence I cannot but look upon every soul you leave under my care as a talent committed to me under a trust by the great Lord of all the families of heaven and earth. And if I am unfaithful to him or to you in neglecting to improve these talents, how shall I answer unto him, when he shall command me to render an account of my stewardship?" Samuel, apparently, responded with a second, more authoritarian second letter telling her that he desired her to disband the meetings. Not backing down, Susanna wrote back a second time, with a pointed conclusion: "if you do after all think it fit to dissolve this assembly, do not tell me any more that you desire me to do it, for that will not satisfy my conscience; but send me your positive command in such full and express terms as may absolve me from all guilt and punishment for neglecting this opportunity of doing good to souls, when you and I shall appear before the great and awful tribunal of our Lord Jesus Christ. I dare not wish this practice of ours had never been begun, but it will be with extreme grief that I shall dismiss them, because I foresee the consequences. I pray God direct and bless you." Susanna continued to lead her unauthorized meetings until her husband returned from London.

With the shining example and powerful influence of Susanna Wesley playing such a large role in her sons' personal and religious formation, it is no wonder that John and Charles readily accepted the spiritual equality of women. More women than men flocked to the Methodist Society meetings by a ratio of two or three to one. In Methodist classes and bands women found a freedom for expression and vehicle for personal improvement and social action that was not mirrored in society at large. There are no Wesleyan tracts that argue for the spiritual equality of women; it was simply a fact proven over and over again in the daily life of the Methodist Societies, classes, and bands. Indeed, often it was the efforts of women that led to the establishment of a Methodist Society in specific Anglican parishes, as Paul Chilcote has pointed out.

Because of their reading of particular New Testament passages, the example of the early church, and the restrictions of contemporary society, the Wesleys initially opposed the idea and practice of women speaking in public religious assemblies. They were given full equality in the more restricted contexts of the classes and bands, where women could lead and testify, but in the more public life of the assembly of the Society — where their speaking could be construed as preaching — women were barred. For example, in May 1743, Charles Wesley examined the Methodist Society at Evesham and left this record in his journal: "The Society walk as becometh the Gospel. One only person I reproved: not suffering her any longer, notwithstanding her great gifts, to speak in the church, or usurp authority over the men."

Yet as more and more women were drawn to the Methodist movement, and were spiritually and personally awakened through their engagement in classes, bands, and Societies, a few women experienced what the Wesleys called "an extraordinary call to preach." A notable example of this sort of person was Sarah Crosby. She was converted at the age of 29 and filled with extraordinary energy for sharing the gospel: "I was 29 years old within a week," she wrote, "when God revealed his Son in my heart, and now I thought all my sufferings were at an end. I labored to persuade all with whom I conversed to come to Christ, telling them there was love, joy, peace &c. for all that come to him." Over time Sarah became a Methodist class leader, and at that time, while she was in prayer, she received a vision of Jesus calling her to preach: "he spake these words to my heart, 'Feed my sheep.' I answered, 'Lord, I will do as thou hast done; I will carry the lambs in my bosom, and gently lead those that are young.'" As she sought to obey this call, Sarah gradually expanded her role as class leader into a more public role of "testifying." On February 8, 1761, more than 200 people attended Sarah's class meeting to hear her "testify." She proceeded to speak, even though it came very close to what could easily be construed as public "preaching." John Wesley soon wrote to Sarah Crosby giving her written approval for her actions, but it was a qualified sort of approval, warning her not to proceed beyond what she was already doing: "I think you have not gone too far. You could not well do less. I apprehend all you can do more is, when you meet again, to tell them simply 'You lay me under a great difficulty. The Methodists do not allow women preachers. Neither do I take upon me such a character. But I will just nakedly tell you what is in my heart.' This will in great measure obviate the grand objection."

In his famous *Notes Upon the New Testament* (1755), commenting on 1 Corinthians 14:34, John wrote, "'Let you women be silent in the churches.' — Unless they are under an extraordinary impulse of the Spirit. 'For', in other cases, 'it is not permitted them to speak.' — By way of teaching in publick assemblies. 'But be in subjection' — to the man whose proper office it is to lead and to instruct the congregation." By this time, the Wesleys were willing to allow that specific women like Sarah Crosby, Grace Walton, and Mary Bosanquet possessed "this extraordinary call" — given to them by the Holy Spirit — and their ministry was affirmed on those terms. Here we see the Wesleys' grace-filled, Spirit-directed pragmatism overruling the prevailing reading of the scriptural passages that effectively silenced most women in their day. As the Methodist movement gradually separated from the Church of England, the Wesleyan tradition felt freer to develop its own tradition of women preachers.

Slavery

Chattel slavery was prevalent in British domains and was another glaring example of social inequality which the Wesleys addressed through their "worldly" ministry. Both brothers had seen the evils of slavery firsthand during their missionary work in America. While slavery was illegal in the Georgia colony at that time, it was a major industry in South Carolina; it was there that both brothers saw the appalling abuses of human rights and dignity that were associated with the slave trade. Charles recorded several incidents of the abuse of slaves in his journal, and concluded: "It were endless to recount all the shocking instances of diabolical cruelty which these men (as they call themselves) daily practice upon their fellow-creatures, and that on the most trivial occasions. . . . These horrid cruelties are the less to be wondered at, because the government itself, in effect, countenances and allows them to kill their slaves, by the ridiculous penalty appointed for it, of about seven pounds sterling, half of which is usually saved by the criminal's informing against himself. This I can look upon as no other than a public act to indemnify murder." Both brothers ministered to blacks, slave and free, in America and in England, without discrimination. In his 1755 *Note* on 1 Timothy 1:9-10, John wrote, "Knowing this, that the law doth not lie against a righteous man; but against the lawless and disobedient, against the ungodly and sinners, the unholy and profane . . . man stealers . . . and any other thing that is contrary to wholesome doctrine. . . . *Man stealers* — the worst of all thieves, in comparison of whom highwaymen and house-breakers are innocent! What then are most traders in Negroes, procurers of servants for America . . . ?"

The Wesleys' active opposition to slavery began to take shape in the 1770s as they came into contact with the abolitionist writings of Antony Benezet and others. In 1772 the case of James Somerset, a runaway slave, which was making its way through the public courts in Britain, also brought the slavery issue to the Wesleys' attention. In 1774 John published his *Thoughts Upon Slavery,* a blistering attack on the slave trade and slave traders. It went through four separate editions in two years. In that writing Wesley not only expressed his revulsion against slavery, he also proposed an economic boycott against slave-produced products such as sugar and rum. He concluded: "Give liberty to whom liberty is due, that is, to every child of man, to every partaker of human nature. Let none serve you but by his own act and deed, by his own voluntary choice. Away with all whips, all chains, all compulsion! Be gentle toward all men; and see that you invariably do unto every one as you would he should do unto you." During this same time Charles wrote a long poem bewailing the evils of "The Slave Trade." Here are the first two stanzas of it:

> Force'd from home and all its pleasures,
>   Afric's coast I left forlorn;
> To increase a stranger's treasures,
>   O'er the raging billows borne.
> Men from England bought and sold me,
>   Paid my price in paltry gold;
> But though their's have enroll'd me,
>   Minds are never to be sold.
>
> Still in thought as free as ever,
>   What are England's rights, I ask,
> Me from my delights to sever,
>   Me to torture, me to task?
> Fleecy locks and black complexion
>   Cannot forfeit nature's claim:
> Skins may differ, but affection
>   Dwells in white and black the same.

On Thursday, December 6, 1787, John preached an anti-slavery sermon in Bristol — the English seaport at the heart of the slave trade. Such a dispute and opposition broke out in the middle of his preaching that Wesley felt forced to conclude, "It was the strangest incident of the kind I ever remember and believe none can account for it without supposing some preternatural influence. Satan fought lest his kingdom should be delivered up. We set Friday apart as a day of fasting and prayer, that God would remember those poor outcasts of men and (what seems impossible with men, considering the wealth and power of their oppressors) make a way for them to escape and break their chains in sunder."

In 1791, as the young Christian parliamentarian and social reformer William Wilberforce (1759-1833) sought to craft and pass legislation that would outlaw the slave trade in British domains, he received a letter of support and encouragement from the elderly John Wesley. It was the last letter John would write, and in it he encouraged Wilberforce in his

> glorious enterprise in opposing that execrable villainy which is the scandal of religion, of England, and of human nature. Unless God has raised you up for this very thing, you will be worn out by the opposition of men and devils. But if God be for you, who can be against you? Are all of them together stronger than God? O be not weary of well doing! Go on, in the name of God and in the power of his might, till even American slavery (the vilest that ever saw the sun) shall vanish away before it.

Wealth and Poverty

In his treatise *Thoughts on the Present Scarcity of Provisions* (1776), John Wesley reported and bewailed the current state of economic affairs in England, which at that time was one of the most affluent nations on earth. "I ask," Wesley wrote, "why are thousands of people starving, perishing for want, in every part of the nation? The fact I know; I have seen it with my eyes, in every corner of the land. I have known those who could only afford to eat a little coarse food once every other day." Why could so many people not afford to eat? They had no work, because those who used to employ them could no longer afford to do so. Why could they no longer afford to do so? Because the cost of provisions had risen at such a shockingly high rate: "food being so dear, that the generality of people are hardly able to buy anything else." One reason for this rise in prices was the booming business of the distilleries, which bought up barley and drove up its price to the degree that the poor could not afford a crust of barley bread. Wesley urged surtaxes upon distilled liquors and other luxury items, so that those profits might be used to aid the poor. He urged the nation to turn away from luxury items, like the landed gentry's fascination for fine horses, that were using up scarce provisions.

The Methodist opposition to distilled liquor and conspicuous luxury is well documented in the various guidelines the Wesley brothers penned for the movement. Serving among the "working poor" as they often did, they saw firsthand the destructive behaviors associated with the growing gin consumption of that day and the drunkenness associated with it. The "General Rules" meant to serve as lifestyle guidelines for the early Methodists urged them to "do no harm, by avoiding evil in every kind; especially that which is generally practiced: Such is, the taking of the name of God in vain; the profaning the day of the Lord, either by doing ordinary work thereon, or by buying or selling; drunkenness, buying or selling spirituous liquors, or drinking them, unless in cases of extreme necessity."

Because they wrote and lived in an age which saw the popularity of Adam Smith (1723-90) and *The Wealth of Nations* (1776), they felt forced to address the evils of runaway capitalism. This critique was manifested principally against the conspicuous accumulation of wealth. It was significantly sharpened by Wesley's willingness to define "riches" in such a minimalist fashion that it included virtually anyone above the level of "the working poor." "I account him a rich man," John wrote, "who has food and raiment for himself, and family without running into debt, and something over." Wesley's approach to riches became increasingly prophetic down through the years. His practical bent took Wesleyan evangelism from the doctrine of sin to the use of money with surprising rapidity. John's exposition of the Sermon on the Mount connected gospel "meekness" with both self-sufficiency and generosity.

His most famous treatment of finances appeared in Sermon No. 50, "The Use of Money." Once again, Wesley sought to steer a middle course, this time between sloth and extravagance. He sought to raise the Methodists up from poverty and yet save them from the temptations of surplus accumulation; hence he coined the famous threefold dictum "Gain all you can, Save all you can, Give all you can," which marked out the way of careful Christian stewardship. The acquisitionist aspect of the program ("Gain all you can") was to be tempered by a suitable consideration of love of self ("Save all you can") and neighbor ("Give all you can"). Acquiring and saving money should be seen as a portion of one's Christian stewardship, and should be carried out without selfish orientation: "Expend no part of it merely to gratify the desire of the flesh, the desire of the eye, or the pride of life" — Wesley's threefold definition of the fruits of human sin. The first two rules found their motivation in the third: "Having first gained all you can, and secondly saved all you can, *then* give all you can."

While "The Use of Money" was addressed to the populace at large, Wesley's sermon "The Good Steward" (No. 51) considered the responsibilities of those to whom God has entrusted many talents — people of the upper class and people of financial substance. The tone and content of the sermon fits well its occasion — the "somewhat unlikely appointment as 'Chaplain to the Countess Dowager of Buchan.'" More typical of Wesley was his strong insistence upon "Self Denial" (Sermon No. 48) as a central feature of gospel piety and spiritual power. By the time he was preaching and publishing "The Wisdom of God's Counsels" (Sermon No. 68), perhaps as much as forty years after "The Use of Money," John had become much more skeptical about "the deceitfulness of riches,"

> A thousand melancholy proofs of which I have seen in these past fifty years. . . . For who will believe they do him the least harm? And yet I have not known threescore rich persons, perhaps not half that number, during the threescore years, who as I can judge, were not less holy than they would have been had they been poor.

The Methodists seemed to be among those who were not "giving all they can" — an attitude "without which they must needs grow more and more earthly minded. The affections will cleave to the dust more and more, and they will have less communion with God. . . . That *must* follow unless you give all you can, as well as gain and save all you can. There can be no other way under heaven to prevent your money from sinking you lower than the grave."

By 1781 and the inclusion of "The Danger of Riches" in the *Standard Sermons on Several Occasions* as No. 87, John Wesley had become increasingly concerned about the issue of wealth. He continued to describe "riches" in a very minimalist fashion: "whoever has sufficient food to eat and raiment to put on, with a place where to lay his head, and something over, is *rich*." The danger of riches is that "either desired or possessed," they lead to "foolish and hurtful desires." Wesley noted "a near connection between riches . . . [and] anger, bitterness, envy, malice, revengefulness, to a headstrong, unadvisable, unreproachable spirit — indeed to every temper that is earthly, sensual or devilish." In his view, riches had become more and more the locus of sinful attitudes and behavior. The sermon ends with a familiar saying: "It is easier for a camel to go through the eye of a needle, than for a rich man to enter into the kingdom of heaven," but Wesley followed Jesus in leaving the door of paradise open — just a crack: "yet things impossible with men are possible with God. Lord, speak! And even the rich men that hear these words shall enter Thy kingdom!"

John's third main sermon in this progression on the connection of sin and money, was "On Riches" (Sermon No. 108), which he published in 1788. In this later offering Wesley's tone has changed remarkably, and the somber mood of the later sermon is easily traced to the changing economic status of the Methodists: "How many rich men are there among the Methodists (observe, there was not one, when they were first joined together!) who actually deny themselves and take up their cross daily? . . . See one reason among many why so few increase in good without decreasing in grace — because they no longer deny themselves and pick up their daily cross."

Both brothers had a lifetime of practical experience working with the poor. Their own early lives — which had been shaped by indebtedness and genteel poverty — gave them an empathy for poor people that went beyond pious paternalism. The Methodist Society room became the locus of all kinds of "real world helps" for the people who came there. People were fed and clothed. Travelers and people fleeing persecution were given a safe place to stay. Dispensaries were established for the distribution of medicine and remedies from John Wesley's rudimentary medical textbook, *The Primitive Physick*.[1] Orphanages and free schools for poor children were established. Society members were taught to read and were given Bibles. They were loaned startup funds, without interest, so that they could pull themselves out of poverty by the agency of owning a small business. All of these "works of mercy" were funded, generally speaking, by people who were themselves among the working poor. Charles Wesley visited the poor throughout his ministry and wrote numerous hymns on their behalf. Here is one of them which expresses well the Wesleyan concern for the poor:

1. The poor as Jesus' bosom-friends,
    The poor he makes his latest care,
    To all his followers commends,
    And wills us on our hands to bear;
    The poor our dearest care we make,
    And love them for our Savior's sake.

2. Whate'er thou dost to us entrust,
    With thy peculiar blessing blessed,
    O make us diligent and just,
    As stewards faithful to the least,
    Endowed with wisdom to possess
    The mammon of unrighteousness.

---

1. *A Primitive Physick, or an Easy and Natural Method of Curing Most Diseases* (London: 1747). John Wesley did not attach his name to this publication until 1760.

3. Help us to make the poor our friends,
     By that which paves the way to hell,
   That when our loving labor ends,
     And dying from this earth we fail,
   Our friends may greet us in the skies
   Born to a life that never dies.

Worldly Christianity

The Wesley brothers advocated and lived out a "worldly Christianity" which was vitally concerned with the spiritual *and* physical well-being of people. Just as they refused to have the scope of their ministry limited by parish borders and ecclesiastical propriety, they refused to allow their ministry to be limited to the spiritual dimension of a person's life. Theirs was a full-orbed ministry which was committed to "doing all the good we can . . . to the bodies and souls of men." This caused the early Methodists to adopt a life of radical Christian stewardship, which took expression in a simple lifestyle, temperance, concern for the poor, and pursuit of social equality and economic justice.

QUESTIONS FOR REFLECTION

1. In what ways were the Wesleys good stewards of the many good gifts God had given them? How can we be good stewards as well?
2. Do you see a danger in riches? In what ways can modern Christians exercise their concern for economic justice?
3. What "social sins" did the Wesleys seek to avoid and to correct? What social ills should modern Christians be willing to address and critique?

FOR FURTHER READING

Chilcote, Paul. *John Wesley and the Women Preachers of Early Methodism* (Lanham, Md.: Scarecrow Press, 1991).

Jennings, Theodore W. *Good News to the Poor: John Wesley's Evangelical Economics* (Nashville: Abingdon/Kingswood, 1990).

Kimbrough, S. T., ed. *Songs for the Poor: Hymns by Charles Wesley* (United Methodist Publishing House, 1991).

Smith, Warren Thomas. *John Wesley and Slavery* (Nashville: Abingdon Press, 1986).

Wesley, John. Sermon No. 51, "The Good Steward."

Wesley, John. Sermon No. 81, "The Danger of Riches."

Wesley, John. *Thoughts on Slavery,* in Thomas Jackson, ed., *The Works of John Wesley, A.M.,* 13 vols. (London: The Wesleyan Conference, 1872), vol. 11, pp. 59-80.

CHAPTER FOURTEEN

All United in Thy Name

AN ECUMENICAL SPIRIT

Is thine heart right, as my heart is with thy heart? . . . If it be, give
me thine hand.

John Wesley, Sermon No. 39

John and Charles Wesley advocated and practiced a non-dogmatic approach to Christianity. As we saw in John's sermon "On the Trinity," for
example, they urged their hearers and followers to embrace the basic Bible
truths of Christianity without becoming enmeshed in disagreements about
what they considered to be religious "opinions." Instead, they taught a
"practical and experimental divinity" which was to be lived out as much
as it was to be taught and thought. In their sermons and their hymns the
brothers Wesley consistently pointed to the love of God and the love of
neighbor — what Jesus termed the "greatest commandment" — as the
foundation of Christian faith. Where this foundation was present, a life of
reconciliation and Christian holiness could be built. They felt that all of
life should be governed by Christian love for God and for neighbor; this
love *(agape)* they termed "the catholic spirit." It is "catholic" in the sense
of being universal, a love that embraces all of humanity *because* of the love
that God has shown and bestowed upon us in Jesus Christ. In the words
of 1 John 4:14, "We love him, because he first loved us." This means there
was at the heart of early Methodism an attitude or theological mood that
today we would term "ecumenical." The Wesleys were willing to see fellow
Christians not primarily as competitors, but as co-workers in the common
cause of God.

One of the earliest expressions of this theological mood was evidenced in the first paragraph of John Wesley's little treatise *The Character of a Methodist* (1742):

> The distinguishing marks of a Methodist are not his opinions of any sort. His assenting to this or that scheme of religion, the embracing any particular set of notions, his espousing the judgment of one man or another, are all quite wide of the point. Whosoever, therefore, imagines that a Methodist is a man of such or such an opinion, is grossly ignorant of the whole affair; he mistakes the truth totally. We believe, indeed, that "all Scripture is given by the inspiration of God," and herein we are distinguished from Jews, Turks, and infidels. We believe the written word of God to be the only and sufficient rule both of Christian faith and practice, and herein we are fundamentally distinguished from those of the Roman Church. We believe Christ to be the eternal, supreme God, and herein we are distinguished from the Socinians and Arians. But as to all opinions which do not strike at the root of Christianity, we think and let think. So that whatsoever they are, whether right or wrong, they are no distinguishing marks of a Methodist.

This "catholic spirit" is not an indifference to the hallmark doctrines and practices of scriptural Christianity. Nor, as we shall see below, is it to be taken as an indifference towards theological "opinions." It is not a squeamishness about theological precision. It is not a kind of theological wishy-washiness. Rather, it is an open-minded and charitable attitude of Christian love with which one regards other Christians and their respective theologies.

Just to finish the conversation, begun above, about the distinguishing mark of a Methodist, John Wesley responded to the question: "What then is the mark? Who is a Methodist, according to your own account?" by offering the following extended definition. Notice how Wesley's definition focuses squarely on the fruits of vital Christian faith by stressing Christian practice and Christian experience. John's reply is nothing less than a montage of biblical phrases woven together to form a practical-experiential, theological whole:

> A Methodist is one who has "the love of God shed abroad in his heart by the Holy Ghost given unto him"; one who "loves the Lord his God with all his heart, and with all his soul, and with all his mind, and with all his strength." God is the joy of his heart, and the desire of his soul; which

is constantly crying out, "Whom have I in heaven but thee? And there is none upon earth that I desire beside thee! My God and my all! Thou art the strength of my heart, and my portion forever!"

A "Catholic Spirit"

The definitive statement of this concept emerged in John Wesley's 1755 sermon by the same title. Based on an obscure passage from 2 Kings 10:15, the sermon used two kings from the Hebrew Scriptures as examples of the kind of godly behavior one should have towards fellow believers. John boiled the issue down to two parts: "First a question proposed by Jehu to Jehonadab, 'Is thine heart right, as my heart is with thy heart?' Secondly, an offer made on Jehonadab's answering, 'It is.' — 'If it be, give me thine hand.'"

Exploring the basis of the first question, Wesley pointed out that Jehu, the devout prophet of God, made no inquiry into Jehonadab's "opinions." And as it turned out, Jehonadab had at least one peculiar religious opinion: he drank no wine. Extrapolating a bit on this holy example, John urged: "Every wise man therefore will allow others the same liberty of thinking which he desires they should allow him; and will no more insist on their embracing his opinions than he would have them to insist on him embracing theirs." It is a clear application of Jesus' "Golden Rule" to the realm of theological opinion. In a similar fashion, Jehu did not inquire into Jehonadab's manner of worship. Manner of worship — particularly when it came to worshipping the Canaanite god Baal — mattered quite a lot to Jehu, but on this issue too the godly person was willing to "think and let think." John put it this way: "And how shall we choose among so much variety? No man can choose for or prescribe for another. But everyone must follow the dictates of his own conscience in simplicity and godly sincerity. He must be fully persuaded in his own mind, and then act according to the best light he has. . . . God has given no right to any of the children of men thus to lord it over the conscience of his brethren. But every man must judge for himself, as every man must give an account of himself to God." Hence, Wesley concluded: "I dare not therefore presume to impose my mode of worship on any other. I believe it is truly primitive and apostolical. But my belief is no rule for another."

Turning to the second issue raised by John's sermon text from the Hebrew Scriptures, what does it mean to say one's heart is "right," and then, on that basis, to offer another person the right hand of fellowship? To address this question Wesley ignores the original context of the sermon text and asks instead: "I do not mean what did Jehu imply therein, but what should a follower of Christ understand thereby when he propose it to any of this brethren?" "The first thing implied is this: Is thy heart right with God? Dost thou believe in his being and his perfections? . . . Dost thou 'walk by faith, not by sight'? Looking not at temporal things, but things eternal?" Secondly, John suggested that, for Christians, this text's question implied: "Dost thou believe in the Lord Jesus Christ, 'God over all, blessed for ever'? Is he 'revealed in' thy soul? Dost thou 'know Jesus Christ and him crucified'? Does he 'dwell in thee, and thou in him'? Is he formed in thy heart by faith?" A third question raised was "Is thy faith . . . filled with the energy of love? Dost thou love God? . . . with 'all thy heart, and with all thy mind, and with all thy soul, and with all thy strength'?" Fourthly, "Art thou employed in doing 'not thy own will, but the will of him that sent thee'? . . . Is 'thine eye single' in all things? Always fixed on him. Always 'looking unto Jesus'? . . . In all thy labour, thy business, thy conversation? Aiming only at the glory of God in all?" Fifthly, "Does the love of God constrain thee, to 'serve' him 'with fear'? To 'rejoice unto him with reverence'? Art thou more afraid of displeasing God than either death or hell?" Sixth, "Is thy heart right toward thy neighbour? Dost thou 'love as thyself' all mankind without exception?" And finally, "Do you show your love by your works? While you have time, as you have opportunity, do you in fact 'do good to all men' — neighbours or strangers, friends or enemies, good or bad? Do you do them all the good you can?" This list of seven questions showed the kind of Christian beliefs and practices the Wesley brothers considered to be essential to vital Christian faith and concerted ecumenical action.

Moving on to the final implication of the second aspect of his biblical text, John Wesley explored what it means for Christians to say, along with Jehu, "give me your hand." In typical fashion, John began by clarifying what it did *not* mean: "I do not mean, 'Be of my opinion.' You need not. I do not expect nor desire it. Neither do I mean, 'I will be of your opinion.' I cannot. It does not depend on my choice. I can no more think than I can see or hear as I will. Keep you your opinion, I [will keep] mine; and that as steadily as ever. You need not even endeavour to come over to me, or bring me over to you. I do not desire you to dispute those points, or to hear or speak one word concerning them. Let all opinions alone on one side and the other. Only 'give me thine hand.'" Secondly, "I do not mean, 'embrace my modes of worship,' or 'I will embrace yours.' This also is a thing which does not depend either on your choice or mine. We must both act as each is full persuaded in his own mind. Hold you fast [to] that which you believe is most acceptable to God, and I will do the same."

Turning to the positive implications of Jehu's invitation to fellowship and concerted action, "give me thine hand," Wesley explained: "I mean first, love me. . . . love me with a very tender affection, as a friend that is closer than a brother; as brother in Christ; as a fellow citizen of the New Jerusalem, as a fellow-soldier engaged in the same warfare, under the same Captain of our salvation. . . ." "Love me," John continued, echoing the *agape* love of 1 Corinthians 13, "with the love that is 'long-suffering and kind'; that is patient if I am ignorant or out of the way; bearing and not increasing my burden; and is tender, soft and compassionate still. . . . Love me with the love that 'covereth all things,' that never reveals either my faults or infirmities; that 'believeth all things,' is always willing to think the best, to put the fairest construction on all my words and actions."

"[S]econdly," he continued,"commend me to God in all thy prayers; wrestle with him in my behalf, that he would speedily correct what he sees amiss and supply what is wanting in me." "I mean, thirdly, Wesley wrote, "provoke me to love and to good works." And, "I mean, lastly, love me not in word only, but in deed and in truth. So far as in conscience thou canst (retaining still thy own opinions and thy own manner of worshipping God), join with me in the work of God, and let us go on hand in hand." On the basis of this "catholic spirit" or Christian love, the Wesleys thought Christians of all backgrounds and persuasion could be and should be co-workers in God's causes in the world.

In the closing section of his sermon, John Wesley distinguished the "catholic spirit" from three things that sometimes pass for it. The first of these he termed "speculative latitudinarianism." We might say: it is not an excuse for being wishy-washy about our theology. Wesley continued: "It is not an indifference to all opinions. This is the spawn of hell, not the offspring of heaven. This unsettledness of thought, this being 'driven to and fro, and tossed about with every wind of doctrine,' is a great curse, not a blessing; an irreconcilable enemy, not a friend, to true catholicism. A man of a truly catholic spirit has not now his religion to seek. He is fixed as the sun in his judgment concerning the main branches of Christian doctrine." The second John termed "practical latitudinarianism." We might call this being non-committal about Christian worship and other practices. Wesley wrote,

"It is not indifference as to public worship, or as to the outward manner of performing it. This likewise would not be a blessing, but a curse." Hence, the person possessed of a "catholic spirit," "having weighed all things in the balance of the sanctuary, has no doubt, no scruple at all concerning that particular mode of worship wherein he joins. He is clearly convinced that *this* mode of worshipping God is both scriptural and rational. He knows none in the world which is more scriptural, none more rational. Therefore without rambling hither and thither, he cleaves close thereto, and praises God for the opportunity of so doing." And finally, Wesley noted, "we may, thirdly, learn that a catholic spirit is not indifference to all congregations. This is another sort of latitudinarianism, no less absurd and unscriptural than the former." Hence, a person possessed of a "catholic spirit" partakes of congregational life through receiving the sacraments, and through worship and membership in a particular congregation, even while respecting and honoring the rights of others to do the same in other congregations.

In the concluding paragraphs of the sermon, John reminded listeners that having a "catholic spirit" means that a person,

> while he is steadily fixed in his religious principles, in what he believes to be the truth as it is in Jesus: while he firmly adheres to that worship of God which he judges to be most acceptable in his sight; and while he is united by the tenderest and closest ties to one particular congregation; his heart is enlarged toward all mankind, those he knows and those he does not; he embraces with strong and cordial affection neighbours and strangers, friends and enemies.

"This," John concluded, "is catholic or universal love. And he that has this is of a catholic spirit. For love alone gives title to this character — catholic love is a catholic spirit." The identification of "the catholic spirit" with "universal Christian love" was made complete by Charles's seven-stanza hymn "Catholic Love," which was appended to John's published sermon. The hymn echoes many of the same emphases of John's sermon:

1. Weary of all this worldly strife,
   These notions, forms, and modes, and names.
   To Thee, the Way, the Truth, the Life,
   Whose love my simple heart inflames,
   Divinely taught, at last I fly,
   With Thee, and Thine to live, and die.

2. Forth from the midst of *Babel* brought,
      Parties and sects I cast behind;
   Enlarged my heart, and free my thought,
      Where'er the latent truth I find,
   And latent truth with joy to own,
   And bow to Jesu's name alone.

3. Redeem'd by Thine almighty grace,
      I taste my glorious liberty,
   With open arms the world embrace,
      But *cleave* to those who cleave to Thee;
   But only in Thy saints delight,
   Who walk with God in purest white. . . .

A Threefold Cord Which Shall No More Be Broken

John and Charles Wesley had been close Christian friends with George Whitefield (1714-1770) since their college years, when all three of them attended Oxford University. Whitefield had been one of the early members of the "Oxford Holy Club," where the Wesleys learned and practiced the rudiments of their spiritual discipline. Charles Wesley had loaned him a spiritual book, *The Life of God in the Soul of Man,* and it became the instrument of Whitefield's evangelical conversion. In the early years of the Methodist revival, Whitefield became a famous mass-evangelist, and it was he who introduced the Wesley brothers to the innovation of open-air evangelism.

As we saw in an earlier chapter, George Whitefield embraced the Calvinistic approach to explaining the doctrines of salvation, including the predestination and particular election of the saved and the lost. The Wesley brothers were Arminians, and strongly disagreed with him on those particular doctrinal opinions. And because they were close Christian friends, who worked together to bring revival to the United Kingdom, this disagreement was painful for all three of them. As they began preaching and publishing opposing doctrines of salvation, the Wesleys and Whitefield fell into controversy which led to public attacks and published theological broadsides in the early 1740s.

It seemed to most people that their friendship was over. But that was not the case. Although they never did agree about the doctrinal opinions that separated them, the Wesleys and Whitefield did not lose mutual respect and Christian love for each other. Over time they reconciled, and by 1749 Charles Wesley could write to Ebenezer Blackwell (a mutual friend of all three men): "I snatch a few minutes . . . to tell you what you will rejoice to know, that the Lord is reviving his work as at the beginning, that multitudes are daily added to his church; and that George Whitefield and my brother and I are one; a threefold cord which shall no more be broken. . . . At Leeds we met my brother, who gave honest George Whitefield the right hand of fellowship and attended him everywhere to our Societies." Whitefield also retained his admiration and affection for the Wesleys, and when he died, on September 30, 1770, in Newburyport, Massachusetts, his will stipulated that John Wesley should preach his funeral sermon at Whitefield's own Tabernacle, in London. His intention was certainly to show his own followers and all the world that he and the Wesleys had reconciled and were to be seen as allies and comrades in the furthering of the gospel. Wesley's published sermon "On the Death of George Whitefield" (Standard Sermon No. 53) is an apt illustration of the "catholic spirit" at work in an effort of reconciliation and Christian unity.

John chose Numbers 23:10 as his sermon text: "Let me die the death of the righteous, and let my last end be like his!" After eulogizing the godly qualities of his friend for ten published pages, Wesley turned to the question of that they should do in light of Whitefield's death. His answer was clear: Whitefield would be best remembered "by keeping close to the *grand doctrines* which he delivered, and by drinking into his *spirit.*" In describing those "grand doctrines," Wesley reminded his hearers: "There are many doctrines of less essential nature, with regard to which even the sincere children of God . . . are and have been divided for many ages. In these we may think and let think; we may [as George Whitefield himself said:] 'agree to disagree.' But meantime, let us hold fast to the essentials of 'the faith which was once delivered to the saints' [1 Cor. 14:11], and which this champion of God so strongly insisted on at all times and in all places." Without saying so directly, John implied that the Wesleys and George Whitefield had "agreed to disagree" about the doctrine of predestination and various related opinions. What were those "grand doctrines" Whitefield everywhere insisted upon? "[M]ay they not be summed up, as it were, in two words — *the new birth,* and *justification by faith?*"

In extolling the "spirit" of Whitefield as being worthy of emulation, John Wesley concluded that George was a man "of a truly *catholic spirit*

— a word little understood and still less experienced." Once again Wesley defined the "catholic spirit" as it applied to his deceased friend: "Who is a man of a 'catholic spirit'? One who loves as friends, as brethren in the Lord, as joint partakers of the present kingdom of heaven, and fellow-heirs of his eternal kingdom, all, of whatever opinion, mode of worship, or congregation, who believe in the Lord Jesus; who love God and man; who, rejoicing to please and fearing to offend God, are careful to abstain from evil, and [are] zealous of good works." Thus, John concluded, "Was this not the spirit of our dear friend? And why should it not be ours?"

Charles Wesley also retained a catholic love and admiration for Whitefield, which was reciprocated by the great evangelist. Charles wrote several hymns for Whitefield over the course of his life and ministry, one of which was presented and then published with John's sermon. The first of the four verses commended their friend's faithfulness with the words of Jesus from Matthew 25:23:

> Servant of God, well done!
> Thy glorious warfare's past,
> The battle's fought, the race is won,
> And thou art crowned at last;
> Of all thy heart's desire
> Triumphantly possessed,
> Lodged by the ministerial choir
> In thy Redeemer's breast.

Roman Catholicism

There existed in eighteenth-century British culture a deep-seated antipathy towards Roman Catholicism. This was based, perhaps, in the stories from the English Reformation and the harsh persecution of the Protestants by "Bloody" Queen Mary Tudor (1515-58). Popularized by John Foxe's *Book of Martyrs* (1563) these accounts of Protestant persecution had a significant impact on the English Protestant collective memory. So deep did these sentiments run that in 1698 Parliament considered and ultimately passed (in 1700) laws that limited the religious and civil liberties of Roman Catholics in the United Kingdom. When this legislation, "An Act for the further preventing the Growth of Popery," was repealed in 1778, anti-Catholic riots erupted across England. These riots were particularly destructive and dangerous in London, where they were dubbed "the Gordon Riots." The city nearly degenerated into mob rule.

Because of their Anglo-Puritan roots, and their birth location in rural Epworth, England, it is safe to assume that the Wesley brothers were raised in the context of this staunch anti-Roman Catholic sentiment. But they were also avid students and admirers of the ancient church, and they aspired to be motivated by "the catholic spirit" of Christian love towards others. And so we find that John and Charles Wesley were remarkably free from the deep enmity towards Roman Catholics that characterized many other Protestants of their age. It was clear that they had major disagreements with Roman Catholic faith and practice, but these were registered in the context of Christian love and a desire for mutual respect and appreciation.

One of the earliest extant examples of this approach is John Wesley's letter to an unnamed Roman Catholic priest, written sometime between 1735 and 1739. After expressing his admiration for the ancient Catholic church fathers and their writings, John rejected Cyprian's notion that Pope Stephen was "the infallible head of the church." This, in Wesley's mind, formed the basis for his disagreement with Roman Catholic opinions regarding the current state and authority of the papacy.

"Yet," John went on to write, "I can by no means approve the scurrility and contempt with which the Romanists have often been treated. I dare not rail at or despise any man, much less those who profess to believe in the same Master. But I pity them much, having the same assurance that Jesus is the Christ and that no Romanist can expect to be saved according to the terms of his covenant. For thus saith our Lord: 'Whosoever shall break one of the least of these commandments, and shall teach men so, he shall be called the least in the kingdom of heaven' [Matt. 5:19]." The Wesley brothers shared this sense of remorse and pity towards Roman Catholics and, as evidence of their concern, they sought several times (with varying degrees of success) to evangelize Roman Catholic populations in Ireland.

John, in his early letter, registered two basic flaws in Roman Catholicism, as it was then constituted, which impeded the vital Christianity of its adherents. The first of these impediments was what he considered the worship of images. Since he was writing to an educated Roman Catholic priest, Wesley detailed his objection to this practice from the Hebrew and Latin versions of the Old Testament. The second failing Wesley detailed in the same letter was that "all Romanists . . . add to those things which are written in the Book of Life." Here John faulted Roman Catholicism for embracing church practices which were based on papal decree or church tradition alone, and which did not have — in Wesley's view — the support and approval of the Holy Scriptures. Under this second head, John gave a list of ten such items:

> I find all the additions following: (1) seven sacraments; (2) transubstantiation; (3) communion in one kind only; (4) purgatory, and praying for the dead therein; (5) praying to saints; (6) veneration of relics; (7) worship of images; (8) indulgences; (9) the priority and universality of the Roman Church; (10) the supremacy of the Bishop of Rome. All these things, therefore, do the Romanists add to those which are written in the Book of Life.

These were practices Wesley felt were antithetical to his own desire to be a "Bible Christian."

John wrote and published a second letter regarding Roman Catholicism during his ministry in Dublin, in 1749. This was phrased as an open letter to a Roman Catholic person who holds some sort of antipathy towards Protestantism. The letter was engendered, to some significant degree, by the anti-Protestant sentiment that the Wesleys' evangelism encountered in Ireland. John began his open letter by asking his reader not to believe "the ten thousand stories" he must have heard about Protestants. He asked instead that the Catholic reader would follow their common Lord's injunction to "judge not that ye be not judged" [Matt. 7:1]. In his next paragraph, John allowed that significant and deep religious opinions separated him from his Roman Catholic reader. Even in the face of these differences, he asked, "can nothing be done, even allowing us on both sides to retain our own opinions, for the softening of our hearts towards each other, the giving check to this flood of unkindness, and restoring at least some small degree of love among our neighbours and countrymen? . . . Are you not fully convinced, that malice, hatred, revenge, [and] bitterness . . . are an abomination to the Lord? Be our opinions right, or be they wrong, these tempers [attitudes] are undeniably wrong."

Wesley conceded that the bitterness and hatred was not all on one side or the other: "I know there is too much on our side also; so much, that I fear many Protestants (so-called) will be angry with me too, for writing to you in this manner; and will say, 'It is showing you too much favour; you deserve no such treatment at our hands.' But I think you do. I think you deserve the tenderest regard I can show." His reasons for this are clear:

every person is a creature created in the image of God, and beloved by God; every person is bought by God by the blood of God's own Son — that makes everyone a person of sacred worth. "How much more," Wesley reasoned, "if you are a person fearing God (as without question many of you are), and studying to have a conscience void of offence towards God and towards man?"

In the balance of the letter John turned Protestant apologist, attempting "as mildly and inoffensively as I can, to remove in some measure the ground of your unkindness, by plainly declaring what our belief and what our practice is; that you may see, we are not altogether such monsters as perhaps you imagined us to be." In this long section Wesley delineated the core beliefs and practices of "true Protestant" faith in a way that would be accessible and congenial to the beliefs of his Roman Catholic reader. These beliefs included: (1) the belief in God the Father, (2) the belief in Jesus Christ, God's only Son, who is very God and very man (including his virgin birth), and (3) the affirmation and participation in the threefold offices of Jesus Christ as Prophet, Priest, and King; (4) the reality of Christ's saving death, resurrection, and ascension; (5) belief in "the eternal and infinite Spirit of God equal to the Father and the Son, to be not only perfectly holy in himself, but the immediate cause of all holiness in us"; (6) "I believe that Christ by his Apostles gathered unto himself a Church, to which he has continually added such as shall be saved; that this catholic, that is, universal, Church, extending to all nations and all ages, is holy in all its members, who have fellowship with God the Father, Son, and Holy Ghost."

At the end of his long list of Christian essentials, John asked, "Now, is there anything wrong is this? Is there any one point which you do not believe as well as we?" Anticipating that his reader would agree thus far, Wesley continued, "But you think we ought believe more. We will not now enter into the dispute. Only let me ask, if a man sincerely believes this much, and practices accordingly, can anyone possibly persuade you to think that such a man shall perish everlastingly?" In other words, Wesley suggested that those who affirmed and practiced this kind of shared basic Christian faith should stop damning each other to hell, and should learn how to practice Christian love and toleration towards one another.

John Wesley acknowledged several caveats to his proposal. Not all so-called Protestants are "true Protestants." They are Protestants in name only, and not in practice. He disclaimed "all common swearers, Sabbath-breakers, drunkards, all whoremongers, liars, cheats, extortioners; in a word all that live in open sin. These are no Protestants; they are no Christians at all." John begged his Roman Catholic reader not to judge the faith of Protestants (or Methodists more specifically) by those who claim the name but eschew the vital practice of their faith: "A true Protestant loves his neighbour, that is, every man, friend or enemy, good or bad, as himself, as he loves his own soul, as Christ loved us. . . . He shows this love, by doing to all men, in all points, as he would they should do unto him." He asked his Roman Catholic reader, "Have you anything to reprove in this? Are you not herein even as he [the true Protestant] is? If not (tell the truth), are you not condemned both by God and your own conscience? Can you fall short of any one point hereof without falling short of being a Christian?" In other words, Wesley urged that his description of "a true Protestant" was nothing else than that of a true Christian; if his reader could not resonate and/or accept that creed and practice, perhaps his reader was not a true Christian.

Assuming his reader agreed with him on what constituted true Christianity, he added, "Let us thank God for this, and receive it as a fresh token of his love. But if God still loveth us, we ought to love one another. We ought, without this endless jangling about opinions, to provoke one another to love and to good works. Let the points wherein we differ stand aside; here are enough [points] wherein we agree, enough to be the ground of every Christian temper [attitude], and of every Christian action."

Based on this common love for one another, Wesley suggested that Protestants and Roman Catholics should act in practical ways: "First, not hurt one another; to do nothing unkind or unfriendly to each other." And as a manifestation of this love, "Let us resolve, Secondly, God being our helper, to speak nothing harsh or unkind of each other. . . . In all our conversation either with or concerning each other, to use only the language of love." Based on the universal Christian love Protestants and Catholics should have for each other, Wesley asked his reader to "resolve to harbour no unkind thought, no unfriendly temper, toward each other. . . . [W]e [shall] easily refrain from unkind actions and words, when the very root of bitterness is cut up." And finally, John suggested, "Let us, Fourthly, endeavour to help each other on in whatever we are agreed leads to the kingdom [of God]. So far as we can, let us always rejoice to strengthen each other's hands in God."

Charles Wesley did not address the faith of Roman Catholics as directly as his brother John did. Like John, he shared with them a love for the ancient church, and its practices and literature. But Charles wrote no extant treatises on ecumenism or reconciliation with them. Like John,

Charles ministered among them in Ireland, and wrote several hymns which sympathize with their lost state apart from the gospel:

> Shepherd of souls, the great, the good,
>   Thy helpless sheep behold,
> These other sheep dispersed abroad,
>   Who are not of this fold.
> By Satan and his factors bound
>   In ignorance and sin,
> Recall them through the gospel sound,
>   And bring the outcasts in.

Charles, however, also had "the catholic spirit." He longed for the day when Christians would all be one in faith and practice and cease their divisions:

> No, they cry, it cannot be!
> Christians never will agree!
> All the world Thy word deny,
> Yet we on the truth reply,
> Sure, in that appointed day,
> Thou wilt give us all one way,
> Show us each to other join'd,
> One in heart, and one in mind.
>
> Hasten then the general peace,
> Bid Thy people's discord cease,
> All united in Thy name,
> Let us think, and speak the same:
> Then the world shall know and own
> God Himself hath made us one,
> Thee their Lord with us embrace,
> Sing Thine everlasting praise.

QUESTIONS FOR REVIEW

1. What do you consider to be the "grand doctrines" that all Christians should embrace and practice?

2. How easy is it for you to "agree to disagree" about less important matters of opinion?
3. Do you consider these essential doctrines and practices to be a basis for Christian harmony and comradeship in doing God's work in the world?
4. How would you explain the Wesleys' concept of "the catholic spirit"? Can you distinguish it from "speculative latitudinarianism" and "practical latitudinarianism"?
5. Why is "the catholic spirit" an important characteristic or attitude for contemporary Christians to embrace in our so-called "post-Christian" world?

FOR FURTHER READING

Berger, Teresa. "Charles Wesley and Roman Catholicism," in S. T. Kimbrough, ed., *Charles Wesley: Poet and Theologian* (Nashville: Abingdon/Kingswood Books, 1992), pp. 205-22.

Wesley, John. Sermon No. 39, "The Catholic Spirit."

Wesley, John. "An Open Letter to a Roman Catholic," in Thomas Jackson, ed., *The Works of John Wesley, A.M.,* 13 vols. (London: The Wesleyan Conference, 1872), vol. 10, pp. 80-86.

Conclusion: The Way of the Wesleys

We have reached the end of our "Short Summary of Wesleyan Theology," and perhaps you are saying to yourself, "There was nothing *short* about that summary!" Believe me, it could have been a much longer and much more detailed exploration. We have only scratched the surface, in a fairly broad and concerted way. If you want to go deeper in this exploration, and I hope you will feel the need to do so, please follow up on the "Suggestions for Further Reading" which were given at the end of each chapter.

In this survey of Wesleyan theology, we have seen that John and Charles Wesley sought — above all else — to be Bible Christians. They sought to affirm and live out the truths they encountered through a concerted study of the Scriptures. Like the Protestant Reformers of the sixteenth century, they stressed salvation (justification and sanctification) by faith. In the way they drew together these truths and in the emphasis they placed on particular ones (like new birth, the witness of the Spirit, and sanctification), the Wesleys made distinctive contributions to the development of Protestant thought. Their willingness to work from the presupposition of the goodness of creation and the intimate linkage they saw between creation and redemption broke with the Augustinian way of doing theology, without dispensing with the doctrine of original sin. They looked instead to God's prevenient grace, which allowed every sinner to hear and respond to God's gospel. The Wesleys were also remarkably foresighted in the ways in which they connected human sin to social injustice.

In their theory of salvation the Wesleys were Arminians, without excluding their Calvinistic counterparts from the Kingdom of God's grace. They firmly believed, as Philip Watson has written, "that all people *can* be saved. All people can *know* that they are saved. And all people can be saved to the *uttermost.*" Each of those words emphasized in italics indicates a Wesleyan distinctive: first, the *universal* offer of God's salvation to all people through faith in Jesus Christ. The second item, "all people can *know* they are saved," reminds us of the "witness of the Spirit"; that internal, experiential knowledge that a person has that she/he belongs to God. And the last aspect, "all people can be saved to the *uttermost,*" stresses the Wesleyan emphasis upon sanctification as Christian Perfection, by which they believed that all of one's life could be controlled and empowered by God's transforming love. This was their gospel, and they proclaimed it in sermon and in song, in the highways and byways of the United Kingdom, for more than half a century.

We have seen that while they were men of opposite temperaments, with differing degrees of loyalty to the Church of England, John and Charles Wesley really were partners in the gospel. They had few theological disagreements between them, though they did take different emphases when it came to explaining the difficult doctrine of Christian Perfection. At one point Charles compared the brothers' fifty-year partnership in ministry to the relationship of an old married couple: "we have taken each other for better or worse," he said.

While salvation (justification by faith, the new birth, and sanctification) was the constant message of their evangelism, Jesus Christ was its center. As we saw above, Jesus Christ and his saving death was proclaimed over and over again, in sermon and in song, so that no one within earshot might go through life without having heard the transforming news about God's liberating love for us.

Their evangelistic, evangelical theology was all about Christian practice. And here the Wesleys made another major contribution: through the way they stressed the lived quality of Christian doctrine. They stressed the Lord's Supper, and other spiritual disciplines more than many Protestants do. They understood the importance of the genuine fellowship of small groups, and seem to offer that as a solution to some of the problems that ail the contemporary church. Both brothers viewed the world and its problems as the focal point of their ministry. They were progressive on matters like race, gender, and social equality, because their theology demanded it, even before it was fashionable to be so.

The Wesleys advocated a non-dogmatic approach to Christian doctrine, which was energized by what they termed "the catholic spirit," or universal Christian love. This did not mean a squeamishness about theological precision, or a naivety about the challenges of Christian fellowship

— far from it. But it did mean that they believed real Christians need to work together to bring real change into the world. To this end, they were determined to see fellow Christians, even those whose theological opinions and practices differed significantly from their own, as allies in the common cause of doing God's work in the world.

I sincerely hope that you have been enlightened, refreshed, and encouraged by what you have read in these pages. But I would not be true to the heritage of my theological mentors, John and Charles Wesley, unless I urged you to put into practice some of what you have read here in order to call people to vital Christian faith and to further God's work in our world, in preparation for the next.

Select Bibliography

I. Primary Sources

Hilldebrandt, Franz, and Oliver Beckerlegge, eds. *A Collection of Hymns for the Use of the People Called Methodists,* vol. 7 in The Bicentennial Edition of the Works of John Wesley (Nashville: Abingdon Press, 1983).

Jackson, Thomas, ed. *The Works of John Wesley A.M.,* 13 vols. (London: The Wesleyan Conference, 1872), widely reprinted.

Kimbrough, S. T., ed. *Songs for the Poor: Hymns by Charles Wesley* (United Methodist Publishing House, 1991).

Kimbrough, S. T., and Kenneth G. C. Newport, eds. *The Manuscript Journal of the Reverend Charles Wesley M.A.,* 2 vols. (Nashville: Abingdon/Kingswood, 2008).

Kimbrough, S. T., and Oliver A. Beckerlegge, eds. *The Unpublished Poetry of Charles Wesley,* 3 vols. (Nashville: Abingdon/Kingswood, 1992).

Newport, Kenneth G. C., ed. *The Sermons of Charles Wesley* (Oxford: Oxford University Press, 2001).

Osborn, George, ed. *The Poetical Works of John and Charles Wesley,* 13 vols. (London: The Wesleyan Conference, 1869).

Outler, Albert, ed. *John Wesley* (New York: Oxford University Press, 1964).

Outler, Albert, ed. *The Sermons of John Wesley,* 4 vols. in The Bicentennial Edition of the Works of John Wesley (Nashville: Abingdon Press, 1984-).

Tyson, John R., ed. *Charles Wesley: A Reader* (New York and Oxford: Oxford University Press, 1989).

Wallace, Charles, ed. *Susanna Wesley: The Complete Writings* (Oxford: Oxford University Press, 1997).

Ward, Reginald, and Richard Heitzenrater, eds. *Journals and Diaries,* vols.

18ff. in The Bicentennial Edition of the Works of John Wesley (Nashville: Abingdon Press, 1988-).

Wesley, John. *Notes Upon the Old and New Testaments* (Bristol: William Farley, 1765; reprinted by Schmul Publishers, 1975).

II. Secondary Sources

Baker, Frank. "John Wesley and Bishop Butler." *The Proceedings of the Wesley Historical Society* 42 (1980): 93-100.

Brendlinger, Irv A. *Social Justice Through the Eyes of Wesley: John Wesley's Theological Challenge to Slavery* (Ontario: Joshua Press, 2006).

Campbell, Ted. *John Wesley and Christian Antiquity* (Nashville: Abingdon/ Kingswood, 1991).

Chilcote, Paul. *John Wesley and the Women Preachers of Early Methodism* (Lanham, Md.: Scarecrow Press, 1991).

Collins, Kenneth J. *The Theology of John Wesley* (Nashville: Abingdon Press, 2007).

Deschner, John. *Wesley's Christology: An Interpretation* (Dallas: Southern Methodist University Press, 1960).

Gunter, Steven, et al. *Wesley and the Quadrilateral: Renewing the Conversation* (Nashville: Abingdon Press, 1997).

Hammond, Geordan. "John Wesley and 'Imitating' Christ." *The Wesleyan Theological Journal* 45, no. 1 (Spring 2010): 197-212.

Heitzenrater, Richard. "John Wesley's Earliest Sermons." *Proceedings of the Wesley Historical Society* 37 (1969-70): 112-31.

Jones, Scott J. *John Wesley's Conception and Use of Scripture* (Nashville: Kingswood Books, 1995).

Maddox, Randy. *Responsible Grace: John Wesley's Practical Theology* (Nashville: Abingdon/Kingswood, 1994).

Rack, Henry. *Reasonable Enthusiast: John Wesley and the Rise of Methodism* (Philadelphia: Trinity Press, 1989).

Rattenbury, John E. *The Eucharistic Hymns of John and Charles Wesley* (London: Epworth Press, 1946).

Rattenbury, John E. *The Evangelical Doctrines of Charles Wesley's Hymns* (London: Epworth Press, 1948).

Stromberg, Ronald. *Religious Liberalism in Eighteenth Century England* (Oxford: Oxford University Press, 1954).

Tyerman, Luke. *The Life and Times of the Rev. John Wesley, M.A.*, 3 vols. (Tentmaker Publications, reprint, 2003).

Tyson, John R. *Assist Me to Proclaim: The Life and Hymns of Charles Wesley* (Grand Rapids: Eerdmans, 2008).

Tyson, John R. *Charles Wesley on Sanctification* (Grand Rapids: Zondervan, 1986).

Watson, Philip S. *The Message of the Wesleys* (Grand Rapids: Francis Asbury Press/Zondervan, 1984).

Williams, Colin. *John Wesley's Theology Today* (Nashville: Abingdon Press, 1965).

Index of Names and Subjects

Index of First Lines of Hymns and Hymn Titles

Index of Standard Sermons